PRINCIPLES OF LEADERSHIP

—

STEPHEN W. NORTHAM, DPA
MATTHEW L. HIPPS, MPA, ABD
HEATHER A. D. MBAYE, PH.D.

UNG
UNIVERSITY *of*
NORTH GEORGIA
UNIVERSITY PRESS

Blue Ridge | Cumming | Dahlonega | Gainesville | Oconee

ISBN: 978-1-940771-97-7

Produced by:
University System of Georgia

Published by:
University of North Georgia Press
Dahlonega, Georgia

Cover Design: Ariana Adams
Layout Design: Corey Parson

For more information, please visit http://ung.edu/university-press
Or email ungpress@ung.edu
Instructor Resources available upon request.

TABLE OF CONTENTS

CHAPTER 2: IDENTIFYING STRENGTHS AND PHILOSOPHY OF LEADERSHIP 27

CHAPTER 3: TASKS, RELATIONSHIPS, AND LEADERSHIP SKILLS 37

CHAPTER 5: LEADERSHIP IN A DIVERSE AND INCLUSIVE ORGANIZATION

CHAPTER 7: SURMOUNTING OBSTACLES TO EFFECTIVE LEADERSHIP   103

CHAPTER 8: PUTTING IT ALL TOGETHER—MAKING LEADERSHIP WORK FOR YOU   111

Preface: Principles of Leadership

The textbook, *Principles of Leadership*, was commissioned by the University System of Georgia (USG) eMajor program. This program partners various institutions within the USG system to provide an affordable, quality post-secondary degree and credential plan of study to meet the workplace needs of Georgia. The textbook will be part of the required material for an eMajor course, Profiles of Leaders.

The intent and structure of the book presents leadership principles by using various authors who would offer students a wider variety of academic research and professional experiences. This broader view, then, would enhance the student experience, providing leadership principles that could be used by undergraduate students in not only their course of study but also their current and future career paths. Three faculty members from participating institutions were asked to co-author this text, bringing together various views and experiences to the basic study of leadership. The contributing authors are Drs. Heather Mbaye, University of West Georgia; Stephen Northam, University of North Georgia; and Matthew Hipps, MPA, from Dalton State College. Therefore, the textbook presents both academic research literature and professionally distinct understandings of leadership in practice.

Given the joint nature of the textbook, each chapter is a contribution by one of the co-authors. This approach offers a variety of understandings regarding leadership principles along with the thematic thread of what it means to be a leader in an organization.

The textbook's structure comprises two parts. Chapters one through four review the theoretical literature and research on leadership. They address topics ranging from what it means to lead from both a historical and current perspective, to differing types of leadership styles and organizations. In addition, these chapters address the on-going and highly debated topic of whether leadership is an innate gift or a learned skill. Last, these chapters end by addressing how leadership needs to be integrated within the organization using the creative process of organization mission and vision building.

The last four chapters present the journey of defining necessary leadership behaviors and how these behaviors must be demonstrated to an organization. The behaviors addressed begin with how to be an inclusive leader who demonstrates constructive actions while helping to create a diverse organization. Next, the textbook considers the difficult leadership task of demonstrating a fair, impartial, and ethical approach to organization conflict resolution as demonstrated in leading an organization in overcoming difficult obstacles. Last, the closing chapter uses several case studies to draw together theoretical and practical techniques in order to demonstrate some of the basic principles of leadership.

1 Understanding Leadership

1.1 LEARNING OBJECTIVES

After reading this chapter students will

1. Discuss the evolution of leadership theory throughout history
2. Understand the history of leadership and current leadership theories
3. Recognize the difference between leadership and management
4. Compare and contrast American and global leadership perspectives
5. Understand the concept and identify the characteristics of toxic leadership

1.2 KEY TERMS

- Leadership
- Leadership of being
- Leadership of doing
- Leadership of service
- Great Man Theory
- Trait Theory
- Behavioral Leadership Theory
- Process behaviors
- Task behaviors
- Contingency Theory
- Transactional Theory
- Servant leadership
- Transformational leadership
- Intelligence

- Courage
- Ethics
- Adaptability
- Toxic/Destructive leadership

1.3 INTRODUCTION

As noted in the Preface, the overarching goal of this textbook is to examine the qualities and characteristics of effective leadership within an organization. While leadership occurs in a vast array of settings, this book specifically focuses on leadership within an organizational structure. To begin our examination, we will explore the evolution of leadership and how leadership theory has shifted and evolved over time. The changes to leadership theory have influenced leaders just as leaders have influenced leadership theory. By looking at the various leadership theories, we will learn about leadership as a shifting combination of traits, skills, and relationships that are called upon at different times to achieve specific goals. We will discover that there is no singular characteristic or model that produces competent and effective leadership. Rather, effective leaders will have to adapt multiple theories to craft their own unique leadership style. In fact, the most effective leaders will assume an authentic leadership style that works for them and can be adapted to different situations and tasks.

After looking into the leadership theories, we will explore key characteristics of leaders and leadership. It is important to note here that although certain characteristics are typically found in effective leaders, no specific combination of characteristics makes someone a good leader. Such traits often occur in different combinations, levels, and people at various times. There is no *right* combination; rather, there may be a *right* combination for a particular moment or for accomplishing a particular goal. We will conclude the chapter with an examination of toxic leadership.

1.4 LEADERSHIP DEFINED

Leadership is an elusive concept. A simple Google search of "what is leadership" produces approximately 3.35 billion results. Yet, if you ask any CEO what skill they would like to see in their new hires, leadership is at the top of their list. Colleges and Universities consistently tout mission statements declaring their aim to "produce the next generation of leaders"[1] and their purpose to "create and sustain a culture of lifelong leadership development."[2] Despite such pervasive and consistent commitments to leadership, a consensus definition of leadership is difficult to come by. Nonetheless, for our purposes, we will define leadership simply as "the action of leading a group of people or an organization."[3]

Expanding upon this definition, it is important to understand three key points:

- **Leadership is an action**: Leadership is not simply a "talking" process; instead, it is a "doing" process. Titles do not determine leadership; actions determine leadership. Whatever your position in an organization or your degree of authority, you have to engage actively in the process of leading your organization. You are able to engage in actions of leadership from any position that you occupy within an organization.

- **Leadership requires a destination**: Leadership requires you to have some idea where the organization is heading. While you need not be the person to determine the destination (the organizational objectives), you do need to have a commitment to arriving at the destination and an ability to articulate the destination to those who are following you. As noted in *The Dance of Leadership:*

    > No one individual can be expected to come up with all the best ideas about where the group or organization should be going. Moreover, having one individual decide on a course of action not only limits the options available, but also limits the commitment of others to the course chosen.[4]

- **Leadership requires followers**: While you can exhibit characteristics of leadership in an isolated fashion, organizational leadership requires followers. Gaining and keeping followers is an essential part of effective leadership.

1.5 LEADERSHIP VERSUS MANAGEMENT

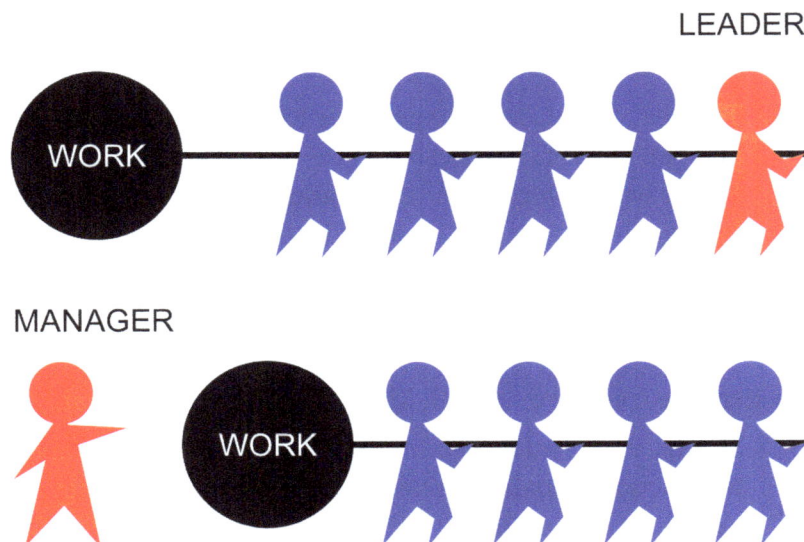

Figure 1.1: Leadership vs Management
Source: Original Work
Attribution: Corey Parson
License: CC BY-SA 4.0

When discussing leadership, we often use the terms "leadership" and "management" interchangeably. However, these terms are not synonymous. They are also not mutually exclusive. At times, a manager may lead a group of followers, but managers are not always required (or able) to lead. Also, a leader occasionally may have to manage their followers, but leaders are not always required (or able) to manage. Although the concepts are different, both roles tend to be needed in truly successful organizations. Here are some ways to differentiate management from leadership.

- Management is task driven. Leadership is mission driven.
  - ◇ Management is about accomplishing quantifiable tasks. The primary role is to ensure that their followers accomplish the task at hand. Leaders are committed to the vision, and their primary role is to see that the vision is articulated in such a manner that everyone within the organization can understand that vision. Managers are tasked with implementing that vision on the ground. Leaders tend to have a 20,000 ft. view of the organization: they are big-picture focused. Managers tend to be more responsible for the day-to-day minutia of making the organization run.

- Leaders take risks. Managers are risk averse.
  - ◇ Leaders take risks and push the envelope to try to move the organization beyond its own self-imposed boundaries. Leaders set the tone, even when that tone is audacious and inconceivable (think Walt Disney). Leaders realize that taking a risk might push the limits of what's possible but are confident that doing so will be worthwhile in the end. Managers tend to avoid risk to help control the possible outcomes. For managers time is money. They tend to focus on deadlines and the need to accomplish short term tasks.

- Leaders have followers. Managers have employees.
  - ◇ The goal of a leader is to get their followers to buy into their vision and feel personally invested in the success of the organization. By the word's very definition, leaders should be out in front and leading the charge for the organization. Managers have people who work for them. Those individuals don't have to buy into the vision or style of their manager; they just need to accomplish the required tasks requested by the manager.

- Leaders are transformational. Managers are transactional.
  - ◇ Managers consider the bottom line. Management is about meeting transactional goals (quarterly goals, sales goals). They have outcomes to meet, and their goal is to meet them. Leaders look to change the paradigm of how people think about the organization. When challenges arise, leaders attempt to find new ways to solve

old problems. Indeed, they look for solutions to problems that haven't yet become problems for the organization.

1.6 LEADERSHIP THEORY

There is no shortage of leadership theories. The question they explore is a simple one: "what makes certain individuals leaders?" These theories have spanned the social sciences spectrum, ranging from anthropology (Bailey, 1998) to social psychology (Bass, 1985); human resources (Hersey and Blanchard, 1988) to sociology (Selznick, 1957); education (Seriovanni, 1990) to political science (Tucker, 1981); and theology (Whitehead and Whitehead, 1986) to business (Zaleznick, 1991) (Rost). Historically speaking, there have always been leaders, individuals who have been expected to provide order and understanding to the unpredictability and chaos of life. The reality is that things have to get done, so we look for someone (or a group of people) to be in charge, or someone we can follow. Figure 1.2 outlines some of the major leadership theories as they have evolved over time.

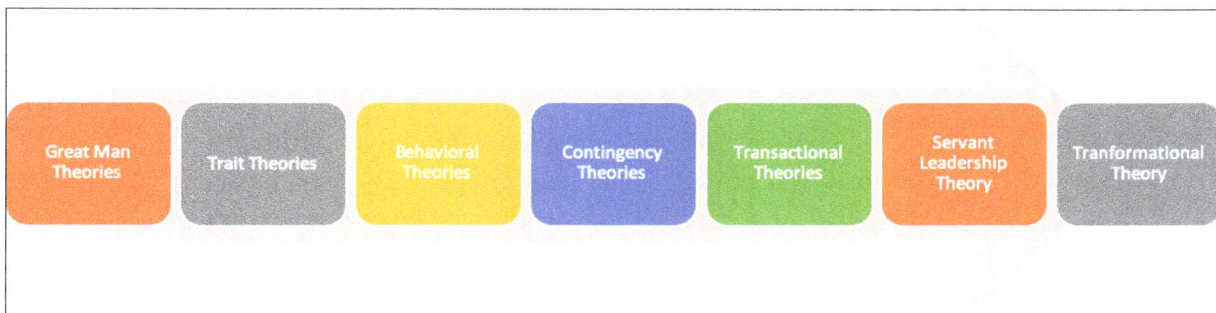

| Great Man Theories | Trait Theories | Behavioral Theories | Contingency Theories | Transactional Theories | Servant Leadership Theory | Tranformational Theory |

Figure 1.2: Timeline of Major Leadership Theories 1840-Present
Source: Original Work
Attribution: Matthew Hipps
License: CC BY-SA 4.0

While our definitions of leadership have not changed drastically, our understanding of how leadership affects our lives and ability to function within societies and organizations has shifted over time. Let's explore each of these theories in some detail.

1.7 THE EVOLUTION OF LEADERSHIP THEORY

Leadership theories have clearly evolved over the last 150 years. They fall under three broad umbrella categories: the leadership of being, the leadership of doing, and the leadership of service. The **leadership of being** includes theories that focus on the innate traits of a leader as the key to effective leadership. The **leadership of doing** theories focus on how a leader behaves and how those behaviors inspire other people to behave. Finally, **the leadership of service** theories focus on how leaders serve those who follow them. It is important to note that some of these leadership models and theories have faded out of relevance in studies of modern leadership. However, these ideas are critical to understanding the foundations of leadership and to serving as foundational layers as you begin the journey of developing your personal leadership style. Though there are quite a few leadership styles, pay close attention to the benefits and drawbacks of each one. This chapter does not intend to tell you that any particular leadership style is the MOST effective. Rather, we consider that parts of each theory can be combined in order to help you develop your own leadership style. We will explore each of these leadership styles in more detail over the course of the following pages.

1.8 THE LEADERSHIP OF BEING

These theories of leadership take the perspective that leadership is an innate quality that some people possess while others do not. **Great Man Theories** and **Trait Theories** both fall into this line of thinking.

1.8.1 Great Man Theories

These theories evolved in the early to mid-19th century. Though a consensus did not exist over which particular **traits** shaped effective leadership, consensus did exist over the notion that only some people (specifically men) possessed this elusive combination of characteristics. It viewed leadership as an intrinsic quality: great leaders were born, not made. These theories posit that such extraordinary individuals were born to do great things and simply wait for the opportune moment to step up and fulfill their destiny to lead. The Great Man Theory centers on two major assumptions:[1]

1. Great leaders are born possessing certain traits that enable them to rise and lead.

2. Great leaders arise when the need for them is great.

According to Thomas Carlyle (the original proponent of Great Man Theory), great men are simply waiting on the right circumstances for their leadership to truly take shape. Carlyle believed that history could be largely explained by the accomplishments of great men who, by virtue of their inherent natural attributes, helped shape the world. He specifically noted that there were six types of "heroic" great men:

---

1   https://www.villanovau.com/resources/leadership/great-man-theory/, Accessed December 2019

Table 1.1: Leadership Hero Types

Hero Type	Historical Example
Divinity	Odin
Prophet	Mohamet
Poet	Shakespeare
Priest	Martin Luther
Man of Letters	Rousseau
King	Napoleon

Source: Original Work
Attribution: Matthew Hipps
License: CC BY-SA 4.0

He noted that these men shaped history because they possessed characteristics that the average person simply does not.

1.8.2 Trait Theory

Trait theory, also under the Leadership of Being, is an expansion of the Great Man Theory. It also asserts that people are born with certain specific characteristics that will yield success in leadership roles. Trait theory, however, holds that there are specific differences in the characteristics between those who lead (or those who take initiative and lead the charge to accomplish a task) and those who follow (or those who operate more responsively; i.e., they wait for others to take the initiative and then they engage). **Traits** are defined as characteristics that are usually relatively consistent across time and cause people to behave and respond in particular ways.

This theory also relies heavily on the work of Thomas Carlyle[2] who noted that "history is shaped by extraordinary leaders, and that the ability to lead was something you inherited at birth and not something that could be developed" (Cherry, 2014). As such, the real challenge was to identify individuals with the right combination of traits to be effective leaders.

1.8.3 Critiques of Trait-Based Theories

Though trait theories were extremely popular at the time, the Leadership of Being perspective on leadership had significant limitations. Not only were these theories subjective, but they also included ever-changing lists of traits required to be a good leader (Ahmed & Bach, 2014). Finding consensus on the traits needed to be an effective leader was nearly impossible because no two leaders were the same. In fact, a leader may utilize different traits that evolve or change across their terms in leadership. Moreover, trait theories did not account for effective leaders who did not possess the "ideal" traits from their lists but still rose to the occasion and became great leaders. They also did not account for individuals who possessed

---

2   Kendra Cherry (2014), 16 Traits You Need to Be a Great Leader, About.com, at http://psychology.
about.com/od/leadership/fl/16-Traits-You-Need-to-Be-a-Great-Leader.htm, accessed December 2019.

the "ideal" traits but failed to become leaders.

Another major limitation of these theories was their tendency to overlook women as potential effective leaders. Leadership was often imagined as the exclusive purview of the most masculine members of society. As such, they focused almost exclusively on traditionally masculine qualities. Women in that era, trained to express more "feminine" (meaning submissive and passive) traits, were viewed as unlikely leadership candidates. Women were therefore overlooked as potential leaders simply because of the traits they were taught (through societal conditioning) to exhibit.

Despite these limitations, trait theories of leadership did offer one valuable perspective on how innate traits can be linked to leadership, and how "nature" can influence how individuals, and therefore organizations, function.

1.9 THE LEADERSHIP OF DOING

The theories that fall under the Leadership of Doing focus on how skills, abilities, and behaviors can be developed and honed over time to enhance an individual's leadership capacity. This idea was a dramatic shift from the trait-based leadership theories of the late 19th and early 20th centuries. The underlying belief of these theories is that leadership capabilities can be learned, as opposed to be being an innate set of skills. These theories fall under the umbrella term of **behavioral leadership theories** and became popular in the 1940s and 1950s.

Researchers were able to link actions of leaders with specific responses by followers. In other words, they found that leaders could behave in a certain way to elicit a specific response from followers. It followed, then, that a leader could learn the particular skills that would make them more effective in particular situations. For obvious reasons, this model of leadership appealed to the masses; after all, it posits that anyone can learn to be an effective leader.

These theories broke behaviors of leaders into two primary domains: process and task behaviors. **Process behaviors** are behaviors that leaders utilize in order to help followers feel included and connected to the group or task. **Task behaviors** are the behaviors that leaders use to complete the actual tasks at hand. The key is for leaders to figure out how to use these behaviors to shape effective practices in those who follow them.

Contingency theories, as adjuncts to behavioral leadership theories, take the position that just one leadership model does not fit all. Rather, leadership is contextual and situational. Leaders must tailor/adjust/adapt their behaviors to fit their followers and objectives. A single leader will need to customize their leadership style to fit each given situation. Daniel Goleman (1997), notes that there are six leadership styles within situational leadership:

Table 1.2: Daniel Goleman's Leadership Categories of Situational Leadership

Leadership Category	Explanation
Coaching Leaders	Help develop the skills of their followers
Pacesetting Leaders	Hold their followers to high standards through leadership by example
Democratic Leaders	Demonstrate communal leadership where decisions are made based on the needs of the group
Affiliative Leaders	Build up their followers with the primary focus on group morale
Authoritative Leaders	Analyze problems and identify challenges
Coercive Leaders	Tell their followers what to do

Source: Adapted from Goleman, D., Boyatzis, R., & McKee, A. (2001). Primal leadership: The hidden driver of great performance. Harvard business review, 79(11), 42-53.
Attribution: Daniel Goleman
License: Fair Use

1.9.1 Critiques of Behavioral Leadership

Again, behavioral leadership evolved from the trait-based leadership models of the early to mid-nineteenth century. Focus shifted from the characteristics that individuals possessed to the way that leaders behaved both inside and outside of their organizations. Simply put, focus shifted from who a leader is to what a leader does. One of the major criticisms of behavioral leadership is that it proposes that many behaviors are important but does not lay out any specific set of behaviors that are most effective within an organization. In fact, the particular behaviors that lead to success vary dramatically depending on the type and culture of the organization. This concept means a set of behaviors that are effective in one organization might be completely ineffective in another. Behavioral theories essentially ignore the need for behaviors to adjust based on the situations you encounter as a leader.

Another important critique of behavioral leadership is that it takes a considerable amount of time and effort (both on an individual and organizational level) to develop behaviors. This leadership model is essentially "trial under fire." The only way to know if your behaviors are effective as a leader is to actually engage in leadership. It is very difficult to test behaviors in a controlled environment where the consequences are inconsequential. Engaging in the wrong behaviors can have real organizational consequences, and leaders who engage in the incorrect behaviors may not get another opportunity (within that organization) to reimagine new behaviors that bring them (and the organization) success.

1.10 THE LEADERSHIP OF SERVICE

Leadership of Service Theories view leadership as the ability to build and nurture relationships. In these theories, effective leadership is related to the ability of leaders to communicate with their followers. For example, political scientist

Richard Neustadt, who studies presidential leadership, noted that presidential leadership is almost entirely rooted in the power of persuasion. In other words, presidents who successfully build trust and communication with their constituents are able to persuade their constituents (to vote for them, to support their policies, etc.), so they are more successful in their leadership efforts. Some of the theories and perspectives that fall under Leadership of Service include transactional theories, servant leadership, and transformational leadership.

Leadership in Action: FDR and the Power of Persuasion

One of the most iconic images of President Franklin Delano Roosevelt is of him sitting behind the Resolute Desk, addressing the nation in his famous fireside chats. In the 1930s, almost 90% of Americans had a radio. Roosevelt realized he, therefore, had an opportunity to talk directly to the American public and utilize the power of persuasion to his benefit. Roosevelt conceived a plan to take his case for expanding government directly to the American people. From this plan, fireside chats were born. During these chats, Roosevelt used simple, accessible language and provided examples to prove his points. He addressed the American people as "my friends" and often referred to himself as "I" and the American people as "we." He played the Star-Spangled Banner at the end of every speech. In order to gain the support of the public, he spoke directly to them. He knew that his best chance to enact his agenda was to persuade the public that his view of America was correct. Roosevelt's efforts at persuasion were wildly successful. These chats increased Roosevelt's approval ratings and were a key factor in his becoming the only U.S. president elected to four consecutive terms.

1.10.1 Transactional Theories

These theories assert that relationships are transactional; in effect, they are characterized by transactions made between a leader and followers. These theories espouse using rewards and punishments. An effective leader will create a reward structure that motivates followers (through their own self-interest) to work towards goals that benefit the organization. These theories assert that followers are not inherently self-motivated; rather, they require structure and supervision to complete tasks effectively. As such, **transactional leaders** tend to reinforce already-existing rules and standards, encourage compliance with those rules, and offer rewards for following the rules. This more traditional style rewards followers when they follow the instructions provided by their leaders (Wamy & Swamy, 2014, p. 58). The style uses contingent rewards for work appropriately done and entails close monitoring and measures of correction to encourage employees to meet accepted standards. A transactional leader creates structure and places values on results. For example, many successful NFL coaches are good examples of transactional leaders. They expect hard work, dedication, and practice, practice, practice. Vince Lombardi, a well-known transactional leader, once said, "the price of success is hard work, dedication to the job at hand, and the determination that whether we win or lose, we have applied the best of ourselves to the task at hand."

Leadership in Action: Transactional Leadership in the Real World

The United States military perfectly exemplifies transactional leadership. The organization is largely hierarchical so clearly delineates between those in charge (leaders) and those who are in subordinate roles (followers). General Norman Schwarzkopf was the commander-in-chief of the U.S. forces during Operation Desert Storm. He was responsible for the command of tens of thousands of troops in both Iraq and Kuwait. General Schwarzkopf's leadership style focused on using the rules and regulations of the military to effectively coordinate military operations simultaneously on multiple continents. He was able to enact this strategy by being a leader who was highly focused on structure, preparedness, and training. Though General Schwarzkopf was known for being extremely hard on those under his command (illustrated by his outbursts at subordinates when mission objectives were not accomplished), he was also well known for ensuring that his subordinates were rewarded for the overall successes of U.S. military engagements. General Schwarzkopf was able to link the military's overall success to the self-interest of individual soldiers. His ability to accomplish the mission and to motivate individual soldiers led historian Rick Atkinson to call General Schwarzkopf "the most theatrical American in uniform since Douglass MacArthur" who provided the United States with "its first battlefield hero in decades."

1.10.2 Servant Leadership

Relationship-based leadership, also called **servant leadership**, shifts the perspective a bit. In his theory, Robert Greenleaf suggests that truly effective leadership stems from focusing on the follower and not on the leader. Greenleaf noted:

> *The difference manifests itself in the care taken by the servant-first to make sure that other people's highest priority needs are being served. The best test, and difficult to administer, is: Do those served grow as persons? Do they, while being served, become healthier, wiser, freer, more autonomous, more likely themselves to become servants? And, what is the effect on the least privileged in society? Will they benefit or at least not be further deprived?*

This theory highlights the goal of the servant leader as ensuring that his followers are taken care of and their well-being is always the top priority. Leaders who are able to prioritize the needs of their workers tend to see higher levels of allegiance from their workers. A 2016 Harvard survey found that employees who enjoy their work, and who continuously gain skills and experiences that will advance their careers, are about 33% more likely to stay in their jobs. In addition, organizations rooted in servant leadership are better able to foster higher levels of workplace community. When people feel that they are all part of a community, they are more likely to see the company's goals and objectives as beneficial to their own personal goals and objectives.

1.10.3 Transformational Leadership

Transformational Leadership is another relationship-based leadership style where leaders work to transform their organizations by motivating and empowering employees to become leaders and take ownership of key organizational objectives. **Transformational leaders** inspire ideas while creating excitement and supportive working environments. In contrast to the first, these leaders operate with less structure but often are known for "thinking outside the box." These progressive leaders positively affect organizational and individual outcomes, including organizational commitment. Francis, et. al (2006) describe transformational leaders as "highly effective agents in the workplace who are concerned with the well-being of employees" (Francis, et. al, 2006, p.78). Transformational leaders typically exhibit the following characteristics: idealized influence, inspirational motivation, consideration for subordinates, and intellectual stimulation. According to Colquitt and Piccolo, "by appealing to followers ideals and values, transformational leaders enhance commitment to a well-articulated vision and inspire followers to develop new ways of thinking about problems" (Colquitt & Piccolo, 2006, p. 329).

Transformational leadership, again, focuses on bringing about organizational change, transforming followers into leaders. The four key aspects of transformational leadership are as follows:

- **Individual Consideration**: the degree to which the leader is in tune with the needs of their followers
    - ◇ **Real World Example:** Your boss recognizes that you are having trouble organizing childcare and allows you to work remotely until you are able to solve the problem
- **Intellectual Stimulation**: the degree to which the leader challenges followers to take risks and question the status quo
    - ◇ **Real World Example:** Your boss tells you that they want you to "think outside of the box" so you present them with an innovative solution to a problem. At a meeting, someone questions your ideas, and your boss backs you up

- **Inspirational Motivation**: the degree to which the leader articulates a clear and inspiring vision
    - ◊ **Real World Example:** Your boss constantly reminds people of the company vision. It becomes part of the culture of your organization to the point that it becomes the mantra by which those in the company live
- **Idealized Influence**: the degree to which the leader sets a positive example for their followers
    - ◊ **Real World Example:** Your boss is consistently the first person at work and the last one to leave. They are constantly assisting on projects and are involved in all aspects of the business. They take responsibility for failures and praise others when the company is successful

1.10.4 The Critique of Servant Leadership Models

The servant leadership model appealed to organizations because it was not based solely on the behaviors of individuals in leadership, but rather on how those leaders behaved in relation to those within the organization. However, there are some who offer that this leadership model is actually about influence and less about leadership. There are a few primary criticisms that plague proponents of this particular leadership style.

The first criticism is that leaders who exemplify the servant leadership style can end up becoming overly empathetic to their employees to such a point as to actually impede their ability to be effective. This is commonly referred to as **compassion fatigue**. Servant leaders are committed to empathy, a commitment that can leave the leader feeling emotionally and physically drained. Most people have limited emotional bandwidth, so their spending all of it on attempting to empathize with and solve other people's problems can become detrimental to a leader's development and productivity.

A second criticism holds that servant leadership actually impairs effective leadership by an almost singular focus on the relationship-based components of leadership. This focus creates an environment where followers are likely to see the role of the leader as developmental. More specifically, it creates the expectation that the needs and wants of the leader are of secondary importance when compared to those of the team members. This dynamic creates a significant challenge when the organization is forced to shift focus, or comes up against a difficult deadline, as the needs of the organization now supersede those of the team members. This cognitive dissonance may be difficult for people within the organization to overcome, thereby leading to a dip in production or effectiveness. In addition, it may become increasingly difficult for employees to see the leader as an authority figure, which could also reduce the leader's effectiveness.

Finally, the most significant criticism stems from those who assert that servant leadership is not well suited to certain organizations. Organizations that are extremely task driven (have to meet stringent financial or product-based markers) or companies that are responding to significant company crises may not be a good fit for leaders who focus primarily on servant-based leadership. In addition, companies that have intentionally high levels of turnover may not be effective landing spots for servant leaders. The lack of focus on employee development and growth will likely play against the strengths of the servant leader.

1.11 THE KEY CHARACTERISTICS OF LEADERSHIP

Good leadership is essential to any organization. According to Montgomery Van Wart:

> In organizations, effective leadership provides higher-quality and more efficient goods and services; it provides a sense of cohesiveness, personal development, and higher levels of satisfaction among those conducting the work; and it provides an overarching sense of direction and vision, an alignment with the environment, a healthy mechanism for innovation and creativity, and a resource for invigorating the organizational culture (Van Wart, 2003, p.214).

An effective leader is an individual who is able to set goals and objectives, communicate them to others, and create incentives for others to achieve the set goals. Put succinctly, leaders are individuals who motivate followers to perform actions that carry out specific objectives (Simpson, 2012, p. 13). Leaders employ and adapt various styles and philosophies to affect and effect performance. Modern organizations increasingly need effective leaders who understand the complexities of a quickly changing global society and can adapt their leadership style to these changes.

It is important to note that although no single set of characteristics (or single combination for that matter) guarantees effective leadership, several traits are widely agreed upon as foundational. They are as follows:

- **Intelligence:** It is important that a leader is intelligent, but not necessarily in the conventional way (though it certainly doesn't hurt if a leader is traditionally intelligent). Often, organizations confuse individuals who are good at their jobs with those who are best fit to lead the organization. While competence at your chosen profession is important, it is more important that a leader possess both industry intelligence and emotional intelligence. Industry intelligence is exactly what it sounds like, that is, knowing as much as possible about all aspects of the industry, and understanding your responsibilities as well as the responsibilities of team members. Emotional intelligence allows a leader to handle interpersonal relationships in the most productive manner

- **Confidence:** Confident people are perceived as self-assured, believe they can accomplish their goals, and (ideally) are able to instill that confidence in their organization in others. Confidence, like intelligence, can be developed through experience. Pursuing mentors (a teacher, boss, a more experienced coworker, or someone who works in your industry) who can act as role models and sounding boards while providing constructive feedback can help build the confidence of budding leaders. Taking on leadership roles, such as serving on committees in your community or volunteering for nonprofit activities, can also help to boost this trait for future leaders

- **Courage:** Leaders who exhibit courage are willing to take risks to achieve and accomplish their goals. Courageous leaders do not seek out risk for the sake of risk; they have the fortitude and awareness to take calculated risks and the ability to handle their eventual outcomes

- **Ethics:** It is not enough to lead; it is critically important to lead ethically. Effective leaders have to keep in mind the right thing to do, even if the right thing is the more difficult thing. Ethical leadership requires that a leader consider the right thing to do through a lens of organizational and personal values, human dignity, and the rights of others

- **Adaptability:** Effective leaders have to be able to adjust to changing times and circumstances. Good leaders are able to help guide their organizations when things are going well. Great leaders are able to adapt their leadership styles to help the organization find success when circumstances are less than ideal

- **Vision:** Effective leaders have a vision or a clear picture of where they want to go and, more importantly, of how they can get there. In addition, they need to be able to communicate that vision to, and get buy-in from, others. Jack Welch, former C.E.O. of General Electric Co., stated it succinctly when he said, "Good business leaders create a vision, articulate the vision, passionately own the vision, and relentlessly drive it to completion."

1.12 LEADERSHIP IN A GLOBAL SENSE

So far, we have focused on American perspectives of leadership. In order to truly understand leadership, we must ask ourselves if leadership varies across cultures and borders. It would seem as though there must be many global leadership styles, as there are numerous types of governments in power across the globe. So how do cultural expectations and norms affect leadership styles?

One study took this question on.

The GLOBE project, conducted in 2014, examined CEOs and leadership teams across cultures and countries. GLOBE researchers were interested in how a society's culture influences leadership behaviors and CEO abilities to match their leadership styles to cultural expectations. GLOBE leadership focused on four key questions:

1. How does national culture influence the kinds of leadership behaviors expected in a society?

2. What CEO behaviors generally lead to success?

3. What are some distinctions between high-performing CEOs (i.e., superior) and underperforming CEOs (i.e., inferior)?

4. How important is it that CEO leadership behaviors match the leadership expectations within a society?

After 70 GLOBE researchers collected data from over 1,000 CEOs and over 5,000 senior executives in corporations in a variety of industries in 24 countries, they found "considerable influence of culture on societal leadership expectations, and the importance of matching CEO behaviors to the leadership expectations within each society."[3]

More specifically, the study revealed six global leadership behaviors used to understand how the clusters perceived leadership, which led to development of a leadership profile for each cluster. In addition, the study identified universally accepted positive and negative (effective and ineffective) leadership characteristics. See tables 1.3 and 1.4.

Table 1.3: Dimensions of Leadership and Associated Behaviors

Dimension	Behaviors
Charismatic/value-based leadership	Inspires others, motivates, expects high performance; visionary, self-sacrificing, trustworthy, decisive
Team-oriented leadership	Team-building, common purpose, collaborative, integrative, diplomatic, not malevolent
Participative leadership	Participative and not autocratic; inclusive of others
Humane-oriented leadership	Supportive, considerate, compassionate, and generous; modest and sensitive
Autonomous leadership	Independent and individualistic; autonomous, unique
Self-protective leadership	Ensures the safety and security of the leader and the group; self-centered, status-conscious, face-saving, conflict-inducing

Source: The GLOBE Study of 62 Societies
Attribution: House, et. al
License: Fair Use

---

[3] https://globeproject.com/study_2014?page_id=ceo_study, accessed December 2019.

Table 1.4: Positive vs. Negative Leadership Attributes

Desirable Leadership Attributes	Undesirable Leadership Attributes
Trustworthy	Loner
Just	Asocial
Honest	Noncooperative
Foresight	Irritable
Plans ahead	Nonexplicit
Encouraging	Egocentric
Positive	Ruthless
Dynamic	Dictatorial
Motivational	
Builds confidence	
Intelligent	
Dependable	
Team builder	
Communicator	

Source: The GLOBE Study of 62 Societies
Attribution: House, et. al
License: Fair Use

In addition, the GLOBE project was able to answer these four key questions guiding global leadership:

- How does national culture influence the kinds of leadership behaviors expected in a society?

  ◇ The GLOBE project hypothesized that societal culture values would influence both leadership expectations and CEO leadership behavior. However, they found that effective leaders actually learn what is societally appropriate within a culture and then lead in a fashion that conforms to societal standards. For example, some cultures (like the United States) are performance-based cultures, and they expect their leaders to be participants in the performance and the success of the organization. Simply put, culture dictates the ideal model of leadership, and the most effective leaders figure out ways to adjust to the relevant cultural norms and adapt their leadership style to fit these norms.

- What CEO behaviors generally lead to success?

  ◇ As mentioned in table 1.3, the GLOBE project identified six global leadership behaviors and 21 primary leadership behaviors of effective leaders. They also found that charismatic leadership is the most impactful leadership behavior. In addition, they found that team-oriented and humane leadership were also effective models of leadership. Autonomous and self-protective leadership were found to be the least reliable indicators of success.

- What are some distinctions between the high-performing CEOs (i.e., superior) and underperforming CEOs (i.e., inferior)?
    - ◇ As a general rule, the GLOBE project found that the most effective leaders are visionary and performance oriented. Interestingly, this model effectively means that the most effective leaders must be able to balance the performance-based aspects of their job while also providing a vision that is compelling to their employees. However, the most important point that the GLOBE project notes is that it is not enough for CEOs to simply possess these qualities; they have to be able to perform these qualities at an extremely high level. The difference in degree to which leaders are able to achieve these goals is the difference between good and great CEOs.
- How important is it that CEO leadership behaviors match the leadership expectations within a society?
    - ◇ GLOBE found that it is extremely important that a leader's behavior matches the societal and cultural expectations found within their organization. More to the point, a leader's effectiveness is directly related to their ability to fit within the cultural norms and expectations of the society in which they are operating. The best and most effective CEOs are able to exceed cultural and societal expectations, while the least effective leaders fail to live up to cultural expectations.

According to GLOBE, it all comes down to how well leaders are able to adjust to the cultures in which they exist. While cultural variations certainly exist, an effective leader uniformly is able to adapt to changing circumstances and utilize their skills relative to the environment in which they are operating.

1.13 TOXIC AND DESTRUCTIVE LEADERSHIP

Effective leadership is often the main reason cited when organizations are successful. In fact, truly effective leaders can take a struggling organization and help it turn the corner to find success. However, ineffective leadership can have the opposite effect. Ineffective leaders can stifle creativity and innovation, demoralize the workforce, and decrease productivity. Even the most effective leaders can make mistakes, but ineffective leaders make repeated mistakes (oftentimes the same mistakes) and fail to correct them. When these mistakes become detrimental to the overall health of the organization it affects what is known as **toxic leadership.**

In *Toxic Leadership: A Conceptual Framework*, Jean Lipman-Blumen notes that toxic leadership is a "process in which leaders, by dint of their destructive behavior and/or dysfunctional personal characteristics inflict serious and enduring harm on their followers, their organizations, and non-followers, alike." Toxic leaders inflict significant negativity and discord within the organization, operate in ways that are primarily self-serving, and use their understanding of the organization to take advantage of it (or individuals within the organization).

Kellerman identifies these seven main characteristics of toxic leaders (Kellerman, 2004):

- **Incompetent**: These are leaders who lack the skill (or the desire) to make things happen within the organization.
    - ◇ **Real World Example:** Jim is responsible for supervising all of the people in his department. One employee, Kevin, is really struggling to keep up with his assigned work. He is constantly missing deadlines, and the burden of his inability to get his work done is falling on the other members of the team. Although the other members of the team are starting to voice their frustrations, Jim thinks Kevin is a good guy and doesn't want to upset the positive work dynamic that he has with Kevin. Jim decides that all Kevin needs is a little boost of confidence, so he decides not to confront Jim for missing deadlines as "he's sure that Kevin already feels really bad." Instead, Jim calls everyone together and gives a speech on the need for everyone to step up and tells them that "everyone needs to do a bit more." He then singles out Kevin for working hard, hoping that this pep talk will inspire Kevin to address his work deficiencies. Instead, Kevin, believing that he is doing a good job, continues to miss deadlines, causing the team to grow increasingly resentful to both Kevin and Jim. Jim's failure to deal with the issues with Kevin's performance caused problems within his team and caused them to question Jim's leadership ability.
- **Rigid**: These are leaders who lack flexibility and are unable to adapt to changing circumstances, ideas or information.
    - ◇ **Real World Example:** Sally has been the CEO of a paper company for the past fifteen years, and the company has achieved high levels of success. However, over the last several years, sales have started declining, and the company has struggled to keep up with the shifting market. Sally has recently hired some young managers who have some innovative new ideas to more proactively anticipate the changing business landscape. These changes would dramatically shift the focus of the company and move away from the tried-and-true methods that have served the company well for the last decade. The new managers have data to support their conclusions and have illustrated that this new shift in the company would likely alienate some of their

oldest customers but would draw in new markets and create new potential streams of revenue. Despite all of this information, Sally tells the new managers to put their ideas on the backburner because the company has always done things a certain way and there is no need to change things that have worked for so long. Sally's insistence on continuing to do things as they had always been done caused the company to fall behind their competition. Also, many of her new managers moved on to other opportunities where they would have a chance to implement innovative solutions to problems.

- **Intemperate**: These leaders lack self-control and do not have followers who are willing to intervene.
  - ◊ **Real World Example:** Bill has a tendency to overreact when things go wrong at his company. He decided years ago that the most effective method of leadership was to tell your team exactly what you are thinking in real time. Bill had convinced himself that this approach meant that at times you might have to raise your voice to really show people you mean business. Bill also believed it was better to say the first thing that popped into his head, as that was his most honest response to unfolding events. Bill believed that his employees valued his self-proclaimed "brutal honesty." What Bill failed to realize was that he had cultivated a culture of fear within the organization. Team members still made mistakes, but they went to great lengths to hide their mistakes so that Bill would not find them out. In fact, the team had stopped pushing themselves years ago, opting to engage only in work where they knew they would be successful so as to avoid the potential of failure. Bill's "honesty" had an extremely detrimental effect on the team and prohibited their productivity.

- **Callous**: These leaders lack empathy and do not focus on the wants and needs of the organization or those who follow them.
  - ◊ **Real World Example:** Kris is generally a pretty good boss and is well liked by all of her employees. The one criticism is that Kris is clearly positioning herself to move into upper management and, in order to impress the higher ups, she focuses relentlessly on their pet projects, despite the fact that her team already has a tremendous amount of work on their plates. Kris is constantly taking on additional assignments because she wants her boss to know that she is willing to go above and beyond to make her superiors happy. Though appreciating the fact that she wants to impress her boss, the team is tired of Kris volunteering their time and effort without consulting them first. The total disregard for

the feelings of her team members have caused the team to distance themselves from Kris, as they no longer believe she has their best interests at heart.

- **Corrupt:** These leaders will do anything necessary to preserve their own self-interest.

  ◇ **Real World Example:** Scott was the new CEO at a high-tech computer firm. Because this position was his dream job, Scott decided he would do whatever was necessary to keep his role. Scott was very quick to take credit for the organization's successes and equally as quick to point out who was responsible for organizational failure. Scott quickly developed a reputation for "throwing people under the bus." Scott began to notice that it was more and more difficult to find people who were willing to team up with him on projects and that his team members seemed to be intentionally avoiding interactions. Scott's ambition blinded him to the fact that he needed his team to succeed, and their lack of trust made it difficult for him to achieve high levels of success within the organization.

- **Insular:** These leaders do not focus on the well-being of entities outside the organization.

  ◇ **Real World Example:** James is a good boss who is constantly looking out for the members of his team. He has cultivated a culture of loyalty within the organization so everyone on the team truly feels like James is concerned with their well-being and happiness within the organization. The problem is that the internal constituents are not the only people who are important to the success of the organization. External constituencies, including the Board of Directors, also need to be kept in the loop regarding the objectives and operations of the organization. James has been adamant that this is "his office" and no one from outside as going to barge in and tell him how to do things. He consistently fails to inform his team of important decisions and his communication of critical company milestones and accomplishment almost always occur after the fact. This mentality bleeds into members of the team, until they begin to distrust the Board of Directors, causing a significant rift between upper management and the rank-and-file members of the team.

- **Evil**: These leaders harm the organization through a combination of physical, psychological, and/or emotional acts.

  ◇ **Real World Example:** Steven certainly looked the part of a Fortune 500 company CEO. His pedigree was impeccable. He had graduated at the top of his business class and had advanced at a remarkable pace in every position he had ever held. He was one of those types who seemed literally born to lead. However, closer inspection shows that Steven had left a wake of destruction in every single place that he had ever worked. Although his results (from a revenue perspective) were undeniable, people who had worked under him had noted that he was a nightmare to work for. He demoralized those who made mistakes and publicly reprimanded people for the smallest errors in their reports. He was wildly narcissistic and believed that everyone was out to get him. As such, he made the decision to destroy people before they had a chance to destroy him. He had lied, cheated, and backstabbed to get to the top, and he was willing to do absolutely anything to stay there.

Terry Price, in *Understanding Ethical Failures in Leaders*, argues that toxic leaders view the rules of morality as not applying to them in the same way that they apply to other people. Essentially, Price (2005) argues that these types of leaders convince themselves that even if certain decisions they make blur the line of traditional morality, good leaders have to make the "tough choices." These leaders give themselves a justifiable moral gray area in which they can operate.

Hogan, Padilla, and Kaiser (2007) offer a more nuanced exploration of toxic leadership, focusing not simply on individual characteristics but instead on a confluence of characteristics and environmental factors. They assert that toxic leadership is actually about the relationship between the characteristics of leaders, their followers, and environmental contexts. They portray this relationship as their Toxic Triangle displayed in Figure 1.3.

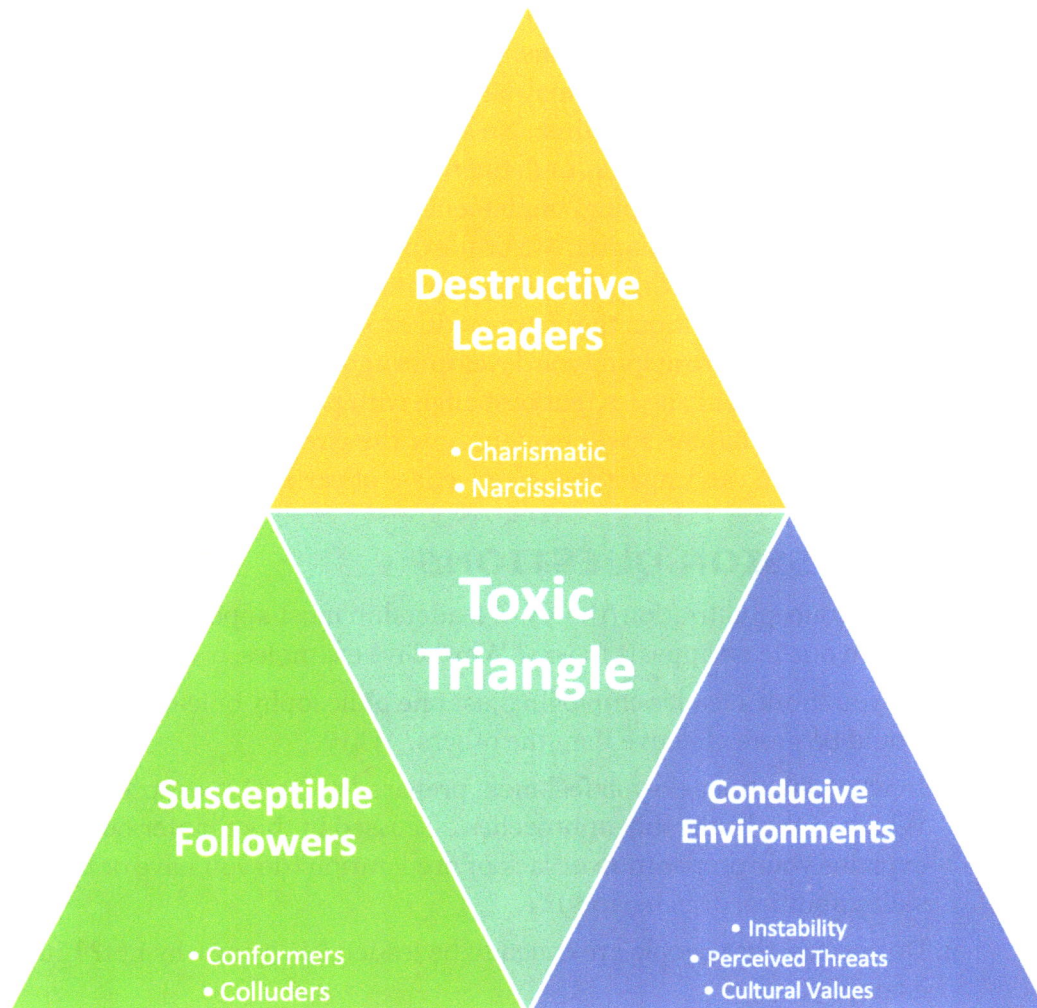

Figure 1.3: The Toxic Triangle
Source: The Leadership Quarterly
Attribution: Hogan, et. al
License: Fair Use

Regardless of the specific style of negative leadership, these types of leaders inevitably disempower their organizations and often reduce the efficacy of their followers. When left unchecked, this type of behavior ultimately leads to the destruction of the organization in a multitude of critical areas. Overall, such leaders tend to erode organizational morale, decrease overall productivity, and cause workers to feel less attachment to the organization.

1.14 SUMMARY

There is a constant demand for high quality leadership in organizations. Effective leadership can influence employees to be the best versions of themselves, leading their organization to operate at its optimal level. However, as this chapter has illustrated, no singular definition exists of what makes an effective leader.

Leadership is relative; there are different styles of leadership that are needed at different times and in different situations. The perfect leader for one organization may struggle in another one. A leader may be effective one year but find themselves struggling to be effective at another time. No singular combination of traits makes someone an effective leader; rather, understanding how to apply one's strengths is a critical component of developing, implementing, and adjusting one's personal leadership style. In the next chapter, we will explore the idea of organizational culture and how important that idea is to create an organizational structure conducive to success. In addition, the chapter will explore leadership more deeply, paying particular attention to helping you develop an understanding of how to match strengths with the leadership styles that best align with particular combinations of strength. In addition, chapter 2 will explore how the circumstances around and within the organization can impact the effectiveness of various leadership styles.

1.15 DISCUSSION QUESTIONS

1. What conceptualization/theory of leadership most appeals to you? Which one least appeals to you? Why? Give examples.

2. Do you think a leader employing just one philosophy of leadership would be more effective than the others? Why?

3. In what situations do you feel most prepared to lead? Least prepared? Which of the leadership approaches discussed in this chapter best explains your preparation or lack of preparation (do you have or lack skills, abilities, or behaviors)?

4. Do you feel that people are called to be leaders? Why or why not? Cite examples.

5. How do leaders become toxic? Give an example of a toxic organization.

1.16 REFERENCES

Al Dawood Ahmed and Christan Bach, "Major Traits/Qualities of Leadership." International

Journal of Innovation and Scientific Research Vol. 3, No. 1 (June 2014): 47-53. https://pdfs.semanticscholar.org/cbe0/29d8a540786bfca174075ba276922887ee4f. pdf.

Alimo-Metcalfe, B. & Alban-Metcalfe, J. (2001). 'The development of a new Transformational Leadership Questionnaire'. The Journal of Occupational & Organizational Psychology, 74, 1-27.

Art Padilla, Robert Hogan and Robert B. Kaiser. "The Toxic Triangle: Destructive Leaders, susceptible followers and conducive Environments." The Leadership Quarterly. Vol. 18, Issue 3: pg. 176-194.

Bass, B. M. (1998). Transformational leadership: Industrial, military, and educational impact. Mahwah, NJ: Erlbaum.

Bass, B.M. & Avolio, B.J. (Eds.). (1994). Improving organizational effectiveness through transformational leadership. Thousand Oaks, CA: Sage Publications.

Burns, J.M. (1978) Leadership. New York. Harper & Row.

Cherry, K. (2016, May 9). What is the Trait Theory of Leadership? Retrieved November 1, 2016, from https://www.verywell.com/what-is-the-trait-theory-of-leadership-2795322.

Cuddy, A, Wolf, E.B., Glick, P., Crotty, S, Jihye, C., Norton, M.I. (2015). Men as cultural ideals: Cultural values moderate gender stereotype content. Journal of Personality and Social Psychology, 109 (4) 622-635.

Gender and Leadership. (n.d.). Retrieved November 7, 2016, from http://www. referenceforbusiness.com/encyclopedia/For-Gol/Gender-and-Leadership.html.

Goleman, Daniel. Emotional Intelligence: Why it Can Matter More Than I.Q. New York: Bantam Books, 1997.

https://www.greenleaf.org/what-is-servant-leadership/, Accessed December 2019.

https://oer.missouriwestern.edu/rsm424/chapter/trait-theory-of-leadership/, Accessed December 2019.

https://saylordotorg.github.io/text_leading-with-cultural-intelligence/s04-12-culture-and-leadership.html, Accessed December 2019.

https://www.forbes.com/sites/darwinatwork/2014/01/10/toxic-leaders-and-the-social-environments-that-breed-them/#13133e5cdac5, accessed December 2019.

https://www.tei.org.za/index.php/resources/articles/ethics-opinions/7213-what-is-toxic-destructive-leadership, Accessed December 2019.

https://ideas.bkconnection.com/why-servant-leadership-improves-employee-turnover-rates, Accessed May 2020.

Kellerman, Barbara. 2004. Bad Leadership: What It Is, How It Happens, Why It Matters,

Kirkpatrick, Shelley A. 2nd ed. Vol. 5. N.p.: n.p., n.d. 48-60. ACAD MANAGE PERSPECT, 1 Feb. 1991. Web. 1 Nov. 2016.

Kotlyar, I. & Karakowsky, L. (2006). Leading Conflict? Linkages Between Leader Behaviors and Group Conflict. Small Group Research, Vol. 37, No. 4, 377-403 • Kotlyar, I., & Karakowsky, L. (2007). Falling Over Ourselves to Follow the Leader. Journal of Leadership & Organizational Studies, Vol. 14, No. 1, 38-49.

Lipman-Blumen, Jean. (2019). "Toxic Leadership: A Conceptual Framework". Encyclopedia of Executive Governance.

Nissinen, Vesa (2006). Deep Leadership. Talentum, Finland. • Albritton, R. L. (1998). A new paradigm of leader effectiveness for academic libraries: An empirical study of the Bass (1985) model of transformational leadership. In T.F. Mech & G.B. McCabe (Eds.), Leadership and academic librarians (pp. 66–82). Westport, CT: Greenwood, 1998.

Pielstick, C.D. (1998). The transforming leader: A meta-ethnographic analysis. Community College Review, 26(3), 15-34.

Roesner, J. (1990). Ways women lead. Harvard Business Review. November - December.

Toxic Leadership - How To Spot It And How To Avoid It". Strategies-for-managing-change.com. Retrieved 2011-08-06.

2 Identifying Strengths and Philosophy of Leadership

2.1 LEARNING OBJECTIVES

After reading this chapter, students will

1. Identify strengths of effective leaders

2. Evaluate leadership strengths

3. Explain the philosophy of leadership

4. Distinguish between authoritarian, democratic, and laissez faire leadership

2.2 KEY TERMS

- Theory X
- Theory Y
- Leadership philosophy
- Authoritarian leadership
- Democratic leadership
- Laissez-faire leadership

2.3 INTRODUCTION

In the previous chapter, the author discussed a number of leadership theories, noting that many examine the various facets of the leadership concept. Further, we reviewed both American and comparative ideas of leadership. In this chapter, we will begin to explore specific theories more in-depth, beginning with exploring which leadership characteristics help us account for effective techniques. That is, this chapter examines what the various strengths people might have are and explores leadership philosophies that underlie success across different circumstances. It will explore strengths-based leadership and leadership philosophy, examining leadership styles and strategies. In particular, it examines Theory X, which leads to an authoritarian leadership style, and Theory Y, which produces a democratic leadership style. The chapter concludes with a discussion of laissez-faire leadership.

2.4 THE GOAL OF LEADERSHIP

All good leaders, whatever their style, ultimately want to contribute to the overall goals of the organizations in which they work. Every leader works within an organizational culture and structure. We must therefore understand a little bit of an organization's background in order to contextualize our continuing leadership conversations.

An **organization** is a group of people comprising a company, a government, a non-profit institution, or similar group, who come together for particular purposes. Each organization has leaders, workers, and employees or volunteers. An entire field of study, **organizational theory,** examines organizations, dissects their structures, rules (whether complex or simple) and culture, while also trying to understand their actions along with the actions and interactions within them. Leadership theory is in many ways an important part of organizational theory, although this book doesn't delve deeply into this field. Finally, **organizational culture**, which can be thought of as the way in which people behave within the organization, informs our views of leadership theory.

Organizational culture is difficult to define, and arguments about what it is form the basis of the field. For our purposes, it is important to note that there are rules, both written and unwritten, that create expectations of the behavior for the leader and employees within the working structure. Organizational culture is defined here as the observable patterns of behavior and expectations that people within the entity display. Leaders can affect this organizational culture, but they are also affected by that same organizational culture.

Even the best leader can be "held back" by a negative organizational culture. For example, a very experienced head librarian was assigned to a new branch library because she was known as a peace keeper. However, after a year, she mentioned that she was glad to be able to retire since the culture in that branch was one of gossip, negativity, and "backstabbing." That is, the employees had created a culture in which everyone seemed to spend most of their time undermining, rather than uplifting, each other. Even a good leader, known to be well liked and able to calm troubled waters, found working in such an environment difficult. A successful leader would try to find ways to diffuse the situation or rid themselves of employees causing the negative work environment, but sometimes the organizational structure makes such solutions difficult. Understanding good leadership begins with understanding the strengths and weaknesses of leaders and finding the best leaders for a particular organizational situation.

2.5 STRENGTHS BASED LEADERSHIP

We should think of people in terms of their strengths; that is, we should think not in terms of people's weaknesses but instead in terms of what they do well and what is *good* about their style. This idea, known as positive philosophy, emerged in the 1990s. To fully utilize this idea, we must understand how to identify and measure employees' strengths in the workplace.

In the 1990s, Gallup pursued a mass poll that examined human talents. A number of themes emerged that people identified as talents that lead to success. Those are identified in Table 2.1.

Table 2.1.: Gallup Poll Human Talent Themes

Executing	Influencing	Relationship Building	Strategic Thinking
Achiever ,	Activator	Adaptability	Analytical
Arranger	Command	Developer	Context
Belief	Communication	Connectedness	Futuristic
Consistency	Competition	Empathy	Ideation
Deliberative	Maximizer	Harmony	Input
Discipline	Self-Assurance	Includer	Intellection
Focus	Significance	Individualization	Learner
Responsibility	Woo	Positivity	Strategic
Restorative		Relator	

Source: Gallup
Attribution: Gallup
License: Fair Use

Now that the study has been completed, Gallup allows users to take a nearly 200 question test that helps them identify areas where they have great potential to succeed. In order to build a *strength*, however, it is necessary to encourage and develop talent through work, practice, and acquisition of knowledge. That is, you take a talent, add your investment into it, and thus create a *strength*. Just as someone who is a natural swimmer must spend hours in the pool honing that talent to become an Olympic goal medalist, so also must a leader take their natural talents and work on them to create a strength.

The four domains of strengths-based leadership are executing, influencing, relationship building, and strategic thinking, according to Rath and Conchie (2008). In order for it to be successful, a team needs to represent each one of these domains. Leaders who are involved in the process will bring a portion of the talents needed, and the rest of the team will fulfill the other requirements. A leader does not need to fulfill all the strengths; rather, a leader needs to recognize their own strengths *as well as the strengths of their team*. Where they lack strengths that their team members possess, the leader should allow team members leadership roles in those areas in which the leader lacks strengths. For example, a certain small business owner, Ella, excels at strategic planning and executing; that is, she understands the customers' needs, plans new product lines, moves inventory in, and does all the appropriate paperwork. However, Ella doesn't excel at relationship building and so hires Leta, an employee who shines at making the customer feel at home, feel welcome, and feel "part of the family." By allowing her new employee to lead in the customer relations area, Ella recognizes Leta's strength in such work that she herself lacks.

You can discover your own strengths in several ways. You can take the Gallup survey linked below in the section titled further reading, or you can take the Reflected Best Self Exercise at https://positiveorgs.bus.umich.edu/cpo-tools/rbse/. Using the Gallup list, you can talk with friends, supervisors, and employees and ask them what they think are your talents and strengths. You can also personally reflect upon your own talents and strengths. This process requires not just your first instinctual reaction but deliberate thought and honest contemplation of the list above.

Once you have discovered your potential strengths, you should develop them. First, you should acknowledge them to yourself and to others. Doing so can be difficult because to recognize strengths is to also concede weaknesses. But remember, we don't all have to be strong in every area. A leader who recognizes that his strength is empathy shows his team that his door is open and he will listen to their problems and worries with an open mind. Another strength he may acknowledge is command – that is, he has a drive to get the job done and keep the team on-task.

In recognizing our own weaknesses, we may employ team members to help in the areas we are not strong in. Also, as the old saying goes, knowledge is power. Once we have owned our own weaknesses, we can begin to address them. John P. Kotter states, "Great leadership doesn't mean running away from reality... sharing difficulties can inspire people to take action that will make the situation better" (Blagg and Young, 2001). In admitting our weaknesses, we make it possible to begin overcoming them. In the example above, Ella isn't very good at relationship building and allows Leta to take the lead in that area. But that doesn't mean Ella should ignore relational issues; indeed, if she alienates her customers, the great new inventory won't be sold. So, Ella should work on her ability to make customers feel more welcome in her establishment. She may never be great at it, but she can always be better.

Strengths-based leadership contends that our strengths underlie our potential for success. Each leader has strengths in certain areas and should play to those strengths. Leaders must recognize areas in which they do not possess strengths; indeed, they should seek to build a team in which all the potential strengths are represented. A good leader also seeks to improve in areas where they may have weaknesses. Recognizing our strengths is key to positive strengths-based leadership. Leadership style, however, also forms a basis for our potential success when viewed as yet another layer of effective command.

2.6 RECOGNIZING YOUR LEADERSHIP STYLE

Each of us approaches leadership differently because we all bring a unique set of strengths and beliefs about ourselves, other people, and the work that needs to be accomplished to the table. Do you think people like work, or do you think most people don't like work? Do you think most people are basically kind or that most people are basically selfish? These thoughts and beliefs constitute your leadership philosophy. Understanding that concept will help you recognize your leadership style as well as the leadership styles of others. A quick Google search will net you thousands of leadership style tests, each with their own terminology. Leadership is a very complex subject, and each chapter in this book will examine it from different perspectives. Understanding what a leadership philosophy is becomes important because it helps us understand the motivation behind different leadership styles. For our first attempt at understanding leadership philosophy, we will examine Theory X and Theory Y.

2.7 WHAT IS A LEADERSHIP PHILOSOPHY?

Every person has a leadership philosophy, which is a set of underlying beliefs about people and their attitude towards work. In order to understand what we mean by this definition, we will examine *The Human Side of Enterprise* (1960) by Douglas McGregor. He explores how managers view their workers' motivations and attitudes toward work. McGregor believes that understanding motivations is instrumental in becoming an effective manager. **Theory X** and **theory Y** explore this major assumption.

2.7.1 Theory X

Theory X contains three basic assumptions:
- the average person inherently dislikes work,
- the average person needs to be directed and controlled, and
- the average person wants security not responsibility.

Theory X presumes that most people don't like to work but find it necessary, if distasteful. Most people would not work if they didn't have to do so. The second assumption flows from the first. People only work because they have to, so they need to be directed and controlled externally or they won't work hard to accomplish anything. Finally, most people don't want the burden of responsibility; they just want to be told what to do so they can get on with it and finish.

The way leaders perceive their workers' motivations influences their management styles. A leader who subscribes to Theory X may view their employees in a negative light. Such leaders will feel compelled to consistently prompt, reward, or punish employees so that they will complete tasks. Supervisors consequently follow closely and carefully what their workers are doing and present either positive or negative consequences swiftly. This carrot and stick approach results in an organizational culture where tangible results will be used as the basis of appraisals and remuneration.

According to McGregor, Theory X-type organizations will tend to have various management and supervisory tiers that are used to provide oversight and guide workers. Authority and control of Theory X-type organizations are rarely delegated but instead remain centralized and lean towards the authoritarian side of the management spectrum. In this model, managers actively intervene to ensure that things are done and workers have very little incentive to suggest new initiatives or share ideas.

2.7.2 Theory Y

Theory Y makes three contrary assumptions:
- the average person does not inherently dislike work,
- the average person is self-motivated, and
- the average person will thrive in positive environments.

Theory Y presumes that most people find work rewarding and satisfying for its own sake; that is, they aren't just doing it out of necessity. Because they find work satisfying, they have internal motivation to complete tasks well. Finally, the theory posits that people will do well in positive environments where they are given responsibility and their skills are appreciated.

Managers who espouse Theory Y will often hold an optimistic view of their team members. They believe in their team's ability to manage tasks to completion. This philosophy often yields a more decentralized and participatory approach of management. Theory Y leaders emphasize a collaborative and trust-based connection between the managers and team members. According to McGregor, team members under this style of leadership will have greater responsibilities, and management teams will encourage skill development. Appraisals, though regular, are used as a means to motivate open communication rather than as a way to exert control over staff members. In a Theory Y environment, employees develop a commitment towards their work and the organization and become confident in initiating ideas.

What kind of leader are you? Are you Theory X (also called authoritarian and autocratic)? What about your boss? Are they Theory Y (also called democratic or social leadership)? What kind of leadership do you think most people prefer? You can take the following quiz to find out: https://www.businessballs.com/freepdfmaterials/X-Y_Theory_Questionnaire_2pages.pdf.

2.8 LEADERSHIP STYLES EXPLAINED

Understanding leadership philosophy is important because it helps us understand the motivation behind leadership styles. Each person has a style, which can be discussed in a number of ways. In this section, we delve into three personal leadership styles: authoritarian, democratic, and laissez-faire. These are essentially based in the philosophy of leadership discussed above. Later in the book, we will distinguish leadership styles through other lenses, but for now we will view these particular leadership styles as responses that people in positions of influence have to their view of people and their relationships with work.

2.8.1 Authoritarian Leadership Style

Belief in Theory X leads to an authoritarian leadership style. An authoritarian leader is a hands-on manager who believes that employees need direction. They believe that employees don't like work and will not be effective or efficient without supervision. Therefore, they manage their employees by frequently dictating procedures and policies. In this approach, the leader decides upon goals and controls how such objectives will be achieved, without meaningful participation of subordinate groups (Simpson, 2012, p. 13). Authoritarian leaders do not encourage employees to communicate with each other and believe that employees should do as they are told. A leader who employs this approach motivates followers by applying strict rules and penalties. This leader has the final word; employees cannot question decisions. Authoritarian leadership overlaps with Theory X because both types of leaders perceive employees as disliking work and needing oversight to achieve goals.

Authoritarian leadership may seem negative (Harms, et. al, 2018), but it can play a constructive role in some instances. Some employees seek more guidance than others; they just want to be told clearly what to do so they can "get on with it." Some people thrive in very structured environments so may appreciate authoritarian leadership—at least in moderation. Authoritarian leadership is often very efficient. That is, people can get more done in a shorter period of time. Du, Li, and Luo (2020) found that authoritarian leadership was particularly effective in creating change in emerging markets. On the other hand, authoritarian leadership can have a negative impact on creativity and innovation, since employees aren't encouraged to deviate from the leader's structure and rules. Finally, authoritarian leadership, since so much power is concentrated in the hands of one person, can lead to that manager's being capricious or abusive. For example, a boss might require people to check their email daily, even when they are home on sick leave.

2.8.2 Democratic Leadership Style

A belief in Theory Y leads to a style of leadership best understood as "democratic." A democratic leader is a hands-on leader who believes teams should participate in decision making for the good of the organization. Indeed, the democratic style of leadership is also referred to as participatory leadership. Democratic leaders are more naturally open to opinions voiced by their employees. These leaders create an open forum for sharing information, and they utilize the talents and skills of all members (Nanjundeswaraswamy and Swamy, 2014, p. 58). While final decisions over a matter will still lie with the leader, democratic leaders believe that people find value in work and can work effectively on their own. They want everyone to be heard, so that everyone feels that their input is valued.

This approach results in higher levels of productivity, with team members being included in the decision-making processes. The style also produces a greater level of intellectual stimulation for employees because everyone is involved in the process of determining a resolution; everyone is encouraged to use creativity and innovation to recommend ideas. This mode of leadership also inspires motivation, confidence, and a feeling of belonging in all members (Nanjundeswaraswamy and Swamy, 2014, p. 58).

Democratic leadership results in greater employee satisfaction and group mindedness. Teams are friendlier, more apt to help and praise each other, and generally happier at work. People may be more motivated and more committed to the work. However, decision making can take up more time—more team meetings and more effort by the leader—which can mean reduced productivity.

2.8.3 Laissez-Faire Leadership Style

This third style is not similar to either of the previous styles. Neither commanding nor nurturing, the laissez-faire leadership is a very hands-off style. Laissez-faire is a French term that means "let it be" or "let it go." Often, it is used to describe a capitalist economic system in which few government regulations control the economy; instead, supply and demand regulate it. Sometimes called "non-leadership," laissez-faire style emulates a minimal-minded government in that such a leader prefers minimal regulation of their team and exerts minimal influence. They do not attempt to regulate their employees nor do they bring them together for collegial decision making. Laissez-faire leadership is non-leadership, in which the outcomes are principally negative. People are not given any direction and they don't know what to do, so they don't do much of anything, which may cause them to become unmotivated.

However, a few situations exist in which laissez-faire leadership can work. If your team is comprised primarily out of motivated self-starters who are already experts in their area, and their tasks don't overlap, then you can achieve good results by leaving them to their work. Highly educated engineers with a history of innovation, for example, may be hired to be part of a team developing new electronic hardware. For creativity to thrive and for them to have the time to complete their work efficiently, it would not be desirable to "look over their shoulders" as would an autocratic leader or "drown them in team meetings" as might a democratic leader.

Each of these three styles of leadership can be successful in the right areas. A military campaign can't have a democratic leader, an app development team can't have an autocratic leader, and an autocratic leader would not do well in higher education. However, the most positive outcomes arise when a team leader employs more democratic styles. To what degree such styles are appropriate is a key decision that leaders must make in relation to their organizational needs and culture.

2.9 SUMMARY

Good leaders are able to capitalize on their strengths while recognizing and compensating for their weaknesses. Leadership philosophies underlie our leadership styles. Leaders can be hands on or hands off, may tend to encourage group decisions or may feel that they need to make decisions on their own. It is important for leaders to understand the different styles of leadership and find the type that works best in given circumstances for given organizations.

In the next chapter, we will examine task leadership and social leadership, both of which bring additional dimensions to leadership. Task leadership is goal oriented and similar to authoritarian leadership, though it is not exactly the same. Task leadership and Theory X do maintain some similar assumptions. Social leadership is people oriented and more similar to democratic leadership/Theory Y. Most leaders tend toward one or the other, some employees need more of one than the other, and some situations need one more than the other.

2.10 DISCUSSION QUESTIONS

1. What are your leadership talents? What can you do to develop those into strengths?

2. What are theory X and theory Y, and which do you find more compelling?

3. What is your philosophy of leadership?

4. Should a leader usually be hands off, or hands on?

5. What is a situation you can think of in which an authoritarian leadership style would work best?

6. Is there a situation you can think of in which laissez-faire leadership would be ideal?

2.11 FURTHER READING

Chapman, Alan. 2020. (2017). McGregor's XY Theory of Management. Accessed at https://www.businessballs.com/improving-workplace-performance/mcgregors-xy-theory-of-management/

Gallup 2020. "CliftonStrengths". https://www.gallup.com/cliftonstrengths/en/253736/cliftonstrengths-domains.aspx

Rath, Tom 2013. StrengthsFinder 2.0. New York: Gallup.

STU Online 2017. "What is Laissez-Faire Leadership? How Autonomy Can Drive Success". St Thomas University Online. Accessed June 2020. https://online.stu.edu/articles/education/what-is-laissezfaire-leadership.aspx

2.12 REFERENCES

Blagg, D., & Young, S. (2001). What makes a good leader? Harvard Business School Alumni Stories. Retrieved from https://www.alumni.hbs.edu/stories/Pages/storybulletin.aspx?num=3059.

Du, J., Li, N. N., and Luo, Y. J. 2020. Authoritarian Leadership in Organizational Change and Employees' Active Reactions: Have-to and Willing-to Perspectives. Frontiers in Psychology. 5 February 2020. Retrieved from https://www.frontiersin.org/articles/10.3389/fpsyg.2019.03076/full.

Gallup 2020. "CliftonStrengths", 2020. https://www.gallup.com/cliftonstrengths/en/253736/cliftonstrengths-domains.aspx.

Harms, P. D., Wood, D., Landay, K., Lester, P. B., and Lester, G. V. (2018). Autocratic leaders and authoritarian followers revisited: a review and agenda for the future. Leadership Quarterly 29, 105–122.

McGregor, Douglas. 1960. *The Human Side of Enterprise*. New York: McGraw-Hill.

Nanjundeswaraswamy, T.S. and Swamy, D. R. (2014). "Leadership Styles." *Advances in Management* Volume 7(2), 57-62.

Rath, T. and Conchie, B. 2008. *Strengths Based Leadership: Great Leaders, Teams, and Why People Follow*. New York: Gallup Press.

Simpson, S. 2012. *The Styles, Models, and Philosophy of Leadership*. Online: Bookboon.

3 Tasks, Relationships, and Leadership Skills

3.1 LEARNING OBJECTIVES

After reading this chapter, students will

1. Name and recognize various task styles

2. Evaluate task styles in practice

3. Name and recognize various relationship styles

4. Evaluate relationship styles in practice

5. Name and recognize various leadership skills

6. Evaluate leadership skills in practice

7. Diagnose the tensions between various relationship skills

3.2 KEY TERMS

- Task leadership
- Social leadership
- Micromanaging
- Relationship leadership
- Administrative skills
- Interpersonal skills

3.3 INTRODUCTION

All good leaders have a common goal: to help their teams perform at a higher level than they would without proper management. Good leaders also enable their teams to meet organizational goals more quickly and efficiently than they would in the absence of leadership. Many different types of good leaders exist; however, a company's choice of leader will also depend on the organization's tasks, culture, and structure. In the previous chapter, we focused on strengths-based leadership and theory X and theory Y (authoritarian and democratic leadership). In this chapter, we continue examining leadership in new ways.

When we consider the best leaders we have known, we probably think of those who both accomplish much and make us feel good to be part of their team. A good leader is kind, caring, and able to get things done. Much like a good professor who both knows the material and cares about their students, a good leader will be able to aid their team members in their professional endeavors while remaining popular with them. In the first half of this chapter, we will explore the facets of task and social leadership along with the tension between the two forms. In addition to using task vs social leadership, managers need skills in order to prosper. In this chapter, we examine such leadership skills. These abilities may be learned since, as we've learned in the previous chapter, leaders aren't just born; they are also developed through the acquisition of skills.

3.4 WHAT ARE TASK LEADERSHIP AND SOCIAL LEADERSHIP?

Similar to the tension that exists between authoritarian (theory X) and democratic (theory Y) leadership, a primary strain occurs between **task leadership** and **social leadership**. This tension typically exists because task leadership is goal oriented while social leadership is people oriented. It may seem that these types are simply different names for authoritarian and democratic leadership, but the overlap between the styles isn't perfect, as we will see. Many leaders would find it difficult to focus on both task and social leadership at once, and most leaders tend toward one or the other. Many studies that have examined leadership behavior (Blake and McCanse, 1991; Mitsumi, 1985; Leonard and Pakdil, 2006) suggest that the various leadership characters may be ultimately distilled into these two fundamental categories. Indeed, a tension often exists between these two distinct forms of leadership.

Task leadership is focused on achieving goals—checking off the boxes, so to speak—while social leadership is focused on the rapport between leaders and teams within the group itself. Sometimes, a strong task leader is needed while, at other times, a robust social leader may find better success. Most leaders find that they use some mix of the two styles; they work on developing in both forms but may value one more than the other or be better at one type than the other.

3.5 TASK LEADERSHIP

We all know people who measure success by how much they accomplish. They may make lists and check off their tasks as they go. They are organized and like structure. They set goals and endeavor to achieve them. Some people keep planners with daily, weekly, and monthly goals. These goals may be color-coded or written on large white boards in their offices. Because they like structure, they feel in control when they can check off a task. The goals that task-oriented people set may be personal, family, or work goals. Task-oriented people find comfort and meaning in *doing things*. These task-oriented people often make task-oriented leaders. We can think of task leadership in several ways: **initiating structure** (Stogdill, 1974); **production orientation** (Bowers and Seashore, 1966); or **concern for production** (Blake and Mouton, 1964). Each of these emphasizes different aspects of task leadership.

An initiating structure occurs when a leader sets goals, organizes job tasks, and distributes the workload. Some leaders who favor this form will also spend time deciding who is going to do which task, in order to make the assignments fair for everyone. Production orientation, on the other hand, happens when a leader is more concerned with product development and other technical aspects of the work. This leader plans and reviews technical documents rather than specific tasks or workloads. Leaders with a concern for production will set sales goals or production quotas (depending on the work), without as much focus on their employees' or team members' various roles in accomplishing the ultimate objective.

These types all emphasize different structural areas, but their outcomes are the same. What these styles share are similar intentions to set goals, distribute work effectively, develop products efficiently, and create working structures that allow groups to achieve their goals.

Successful task-oriented leaders share a number of skills:

- *Prioritizing tasks.* Leaders must be able to discern which tasks are more important and assist their team in creating plans to complete these assignments. These jobs may be sorted by deadline, complexity, or some other principle (depending on the type of work). However, prioritization can also change depending on a task's urgency, so leaders must re-evaluate regularly and strategically.

- *Time Management.* Leaders must not only manage their own time but also help their team members manage their time as well. Doing so may involve shared schedules or having subordinates submit regular progress updates.

- *Delegate.* Leaders must be willing to delegate; that is, they must be willing to give a task to a team member and allow them to complete it without **micromanaging** that person. Micromanaging is directing every detail of a project and how to accomplish that project. Leaders must be able to delegate tasks based on skillsets in the team so that each team member is maximally productive.

- *Communication.* Leaders must clearly communicate their expectations as well as the task priorities, deadlines, and the job duties of each team member. Doing so may involve regular individual or group meetings, shared online calendars, or regular memos or emails.

Task leaders can be both the visionaries who set large policy goals and project managers who achieve such objectives. Task leaders may be more authoritarian (theory X) or democratic (theory Y) in their approach; that is, they may make decisions with input from their teams, or they may avoid employee input. Task leaders are efficient and get the work done, but they sometimes overlook the well-being of their teams and may be somewhat **autocratic**, that is, somewhat authoritarian and controlling. For example, Martha Stewart is meticulous and attends to every detail of her media empire. She is known for being a perfectionist who is convinced that her way is the only "right way." Working for her means working in a highly regimented workplace, where she alone determines the organization's work structure. However, all task leaders are not necessarily authoritarian or autocratic. For example, a volunteer organization may have a leader who decides which tasks need to be completed and then asks for volunteers to complete them, allowing the workers to use their own processes. In this case, the leader doesn't interfere in the activity unless they are asked for help in creating efficient processes.

3.6 SOCIAL LEADERSHIP

Social leadership, sometimes called **relationship leadership**, is focused less on tasks and more on people and the relationships between individuals. Social leaders are focused less on *doing*—as are task leaders—and more on being in the moment with the people around them. Such leaders want everyone to feel comfortable and happy. To that end, they are very focused on the people within their organizations and how those people feel. For example, these types of leaders are concerned with the private lives and happiness of their friends and colleagues. They also want to be connected to others and believe that interrupting assigned tasks for a pleasant chat brings more satisfaction than does completing the tasks themselves.

While social leaders understand that tasks are important, they believe the best way to achieve those tasks is by focusing on relationships. They want their team to feel comfortable and happy with others, themselves, and the tasks at hand. We can think of social leadership in several ways: **consideration behavior** (Stogdill, 1974); **employee orientation** (Bowers and Seashore, 1966); or **concern for people** (Blake and Mouton, 1964). Each of these concepts emphasizes different aspects of social leadership.

Consideration behavior emphasizes building respect, trust, friendship, compassion, and camaraderie between the leader, their team, and team members. Leaders with this orientation want everyone to "get along;" more than that, though, they want everyone to be friendly. These individuals are especially concerned with their workplace's overall tone. Such leaders want everyone to look forward to coming to work. They may also encourage activities like passing around cards and taking up collections when fellow workers have new babies or suffer losses. Consideration-oriented leaders are further characterized by actions such as making the rounds in the morning to have a short chat with each employee, or buying lunch for the team.

Employee orientation focuses on individuals and their unique qualities as people. These leaders will worry about each subordinate's particular needs. Such leaders may assign work based on employee preferences. This concern for people orientation also takes on a broader definition. Leaders of this type additionally concentrate on building rapport, issuing fair salaries and workloads, and perpetuating good relations between people.

Successful relationship-oriented social leaders share a number of skills:

- **Building Rapport**: Leaders focus on supporting relationships between their employees, themselves, and their teams. They focus on employees as people and chat about topics that aren't work related. These leaders take interest in the personal lives of their employees.

- **Positive Feedback:** Leaders give their employees positive feedback to support a positive workplace while maintaining high standards and discouraging negative behavior and outcomes.

- **Collaborative Decision Making:** Leaders model appropriate team collaboration from the top. That is, they will make decisions about tasks, goals, outcomes, and workload collaboratively, with input from the team as a whole.

- **Flexibility**: Leaders must be flexible in drawing a variety of people and personalities into the group conversation. Everyone is not the same; many are task-oriented, some are more hesitant to put their views forward, and others are not as social. Social leaders must recognize that not all team members will respond the same way in a group setting.

- **Team Building**: Leaders will focus on teambuilding and promoting relationships among their employees, not just between themselves and the employees.

Social leaders can sometimes lose sight of organizational goals in favor of relationships and helping to develop individuals' skills. Moreover, such leaders rely on loyalty in their employees and can sometimes feel hurt or react negatively when employees are perceived as disloyal or disagree with the leader. While democratic leadership can contribute to social leadership, this form does not perfectly overlap with Theory Y. Nevertheless, such leaders are very successful in encouraging a pleasant and smoothly operating workplace, and their teams usually rank their workplace environment highly.

3.7 COMBINING TASK AND SOCIAL LEADERSHIP

Most people aren't solely one type of leader or the other. Instead, leaders fall somewhere along a continuum that has task leadership on one end and relationship leadership on the other.

Task Leadership ———————————————————— Social Leadership

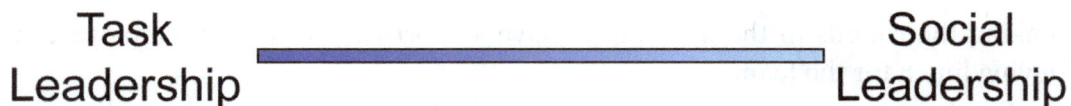

Figure 3.1: Leadership Continuum
Source: Original Work
Attribution: Corey Parson
License: CC BY-SA 4.0

This juncture is where you find your best leaders, that is, those who combine the best aspects of both types. The best leaders integrate these two styles and can move from one to the other in response to team, organizational, and situational needs. For example, in a new business, the leader must focus on task-related skills to give their followers clear goals, while also providing social leadership when uncertainty is present. When setting up a new restaurant, then, it is important that the tasks of each new employee—chef, bar manager, servers, and others—are clear so that everyone knows what they should be doing. Does the chef order all fruits, or does the bar manager have responsibility for making sure there are enough limes for cocktails? Does the service manager have responsibility for glass inventory as well as service wear, like plates and cutlery, or does the bar manager inventory the glassware? A task-oriented manager must make these decisions and make tasks clear to all the new employees, in order to avoid uncertainty and to ensure everything gets done efficiently—and so that they don't order too many limes and not enough glasses to use them in!

Some people want more task leadership from their leaders so they may be very frustrated when they don't get it. In addition, these people can become very distracted when their boss or colleagues stop by to chat about the weather in the middle of a complex task. Others, however, will find task management without social leadership sterile and unfulfilling. These people need to feel connected to their work, happy with their bosses, and united with other members of the team in reaching shared goals. A good leader will assess what their employees need and try to find ways to give that to them. Former Westpac Bank CEO Gail Kelly says, "[Good leadership] … should be about looking to catch people doing the right thing, one that is not selfish or quick to judge; it should be one that is prepared to walk in other people's shoes, one that is prepared to listen" (Kimmorly, 2017).

A good leader recognizes when task leadership is required and when social leadership is required. Sometimes, the carrot is the best motivation; at others, the stick is better. A good leader recognizes what carrot and stick combination will enable their team to rise to new heights of performance.

An ineffective leader will display the negative traits of both leadership aspects. For instance, such a leader may focus on tasks but fail to communicate clear goals. They may also micromanage their employees, sending the message that they cannot be trusted. An ineffective leader may ignore employees' personal strengths and needs, assigning tasks better suited to other employees. They might fail to assess the feelings of others; fall into autocratic decision patterns and make decrees; and be inflexible in their relationships, expectations, and schedules. This leader may be unrealistic in their goals and unaware of how production processes work. This leader will assume their employees work the same as they themselves do so will grow angry when faced with disagreement by their team. However, an effective leader shifts between the two leadership forms and is perceptive enough to know what each team member needs in order to flourish. In combining these aspects of leadership, an effective manager ensures success.

3.8 LEADERSHIP SKILLS

Everyone needs skills to succeed. Even with something as simple as sewing on a button, if you haven't got the skills, you will find the process difficult and frustrating. The same is true of leadership; leaders need to possess certain skills. If you do a quick internet search on leadership skills, you will find thousands upon thousands of sites, all claiming to list needed leadership skills and many offering to train you in those skills. Nonetheless, historically, academics and researchers have focused more on leadership traits (see chapter 1) than on skills. Only recently has academic literature shifted its focus to the skills needed to be an effective leader. However, these have not been focused upon by academics as much as have other aspects of leadership. In fact, leadership *traits* have been discussed much more often. It's only recently that we have begun to recognize a skills approach.

According to Robert Katz (1974), leadership skills enable people to influence other people. Katz says, "a skill implies an ability which can be developed, not necessarily inborn, and which is manifested in performance, not merely in potential" (Katz, 1974). Leadership skills can be *learned*; that is, most people don't emerge from school as fully formed leaders. This section will review three leadership skills approaches from the following experts: Katz; Michael Mumford, et. al (2000); and Peter Northhouse (2012).

3.9 ROBERT KATZ'S THREE-SKILL APPROACH

Leaders are those who direct other people and are responsible for certain task outcomes within an organization. According to Katz, in order to accomplish these goals, leaders must possess three types of skills: **technical**, **human**, and **conceptual.**

3.9.1 Technical Skills

Katz states that "technical skill implies an understanding of, and proficiency in, a specific kind of activity, particularly one involving methods, processes, procedures, or techniques" (Katz, 1974). Technical skills of a software developer involve knowing software languages and computer skills, for example. Technical skills are specialized knowledge, techniques and abilities within one's own specialty. Technical skills are concrete skills that a leader needs in order to be successful.

3.9.2 Human Skills

Human skills, on the other hand, are less concrete. These skills relate back to the social leader discussed earlier in this chapter. Indeed, human skill is a leader's ability to work with others and build collegiality, to motivate people and teams. Leaders with human skills understand their own beliefs and biases and are flexible enough to understand that not everyone thinks and works as they do. Human skills must be continuously practiced; they "cannot be a 'sometimes' thing'" (Katz, 1974). In fact, Katz contends that the *absence* of human skills is easier to see than their presence. Leaders who ignore the human or social aspects of their job and focus only on tasks will not be effective. People matter, too.

3.9.3 Conceptual Skills

Conceptual skills are the least concrete of all. Katz contends that conceptual skills involve the ability to see the enterprise as a whole includes recognizing how the various functions of the organization depend on one another; how changes in any one part affect all the others; and it extends to visualizing the relationship to the industry and community, as well as to the nation's political, social, and economic forces as a whole (Katz, 1974).

Overall success of the business depends on the conceptual leaders' skills at the top. For example, Apple's success is said to be founded most of all on Steve Jobs' visionary leadership; when Jobs died, the business community's perception was that the company foundered while searching for a new vision before bouncing back in terms of sales after reorienting. The success of the whole enterprise relies upon conceptual skill. It is necessary to be visionary about not only products, but also production methods, labor relations, human capital, and so on. The three skills approach is one way to examine the skills that an effective leader needs, but there are others as well.

3.10 THE MUMFORD, ZACCARO, HARDING, ET. AL THREE COMPETENCIES APPROACH

Mumford, et. al (2000) argue that good leaders have three "competencies": individual attributes, career experiences, and environmental influences. These competencies can contribute to positive outcomes.

3.10.1 Leader Competencies

Leader competencies, the first type of competencies named by Mumford, et. al, include several sub-competencies: problem solving skills, social judgment skills, and knowledge.

Problem solving skills most closely align with Katz's conceptual skills. Hard to define, these skills allow leaders to determine the relative importance of issues and tasks, develop solutions, and "think outside the box."

Social judgment skills allow leaders to understand their team and the social systems in which they exist. These skills allow leaders to work with others to make sense of issues, solve problems, and manage people. Included in this skill set are leaders' willingness to consider others' perspectives; being flexible and open to change; and being good social performers, meaning they must be able to persuade and communicate their ideas to others in the hierarchy.

Good leaders must also be knowledgeable; more than that, they must be willing and able to learn knew information and organize it mentally in order to make sense of it. In fact, the most effective leaders consider themselves to be life-long learners, which includes their ability to also learn from the past. Knowledge allows leaders to make sense of and avoid perpetuating past errors.

3.10.2 Leaders' Individual Attributes

Mumford and his coauthors also identified four personal attributes of leaders that influence their competencies: general cognitive ability, crystallized cognitive ability, motivation, and personality.

General cognitive ability relates to memory, information processing, learning, intellectual ability, and critical thinking skills. These traits influence a leader's ability to gain knowledge.

Crystallized cognitive ability means that experience leads to intelligence; that is, as we age and gain experiences, we acquire abilities particularly related to social judgment skills, conceptual ability, and problem-solving skills.

In regards to motivation, first, many people are not motivated to lead. They don't want to be leaders and, when thrust into that role, will not do well. Second, leaders must be willing to bring pressure to bear upon others and take a dominate role in a group. If they do not want to do so, they will not function well. Finally, leaders must be willing to contribute for the good of the whole, not just their team. For example, if your division needs a new assistant but another division can demonstrate that they have a greater need, sometimes you will need to step back for the greater good of the whole organization.

Finally, personality in particular influences our social competencies. Leaders should be open, curious, and adaptable. It also helps if they like people and can let their team shine without taking all the credit.

3.10.3 Experiences

Leaders with these attributes and competencies will be successful at problem solving and in performance measures. But, according to Mumford, et. al, career experience and environmental experience also enhance a potential leader's ability to lead effectively.

Many career assignments offer opportunities for individuals to develop people skills or problem-solving capabilities. Many individuals are not born with these skills so must make an effort to learn them through work experience. This is why universities, for example, send promising faculty members with the drive and motivation to be leaders to leadership academies and other training events.

Moreover, some environmental factors will affect leadership outcomes, according to Mumford, et. al, even highly skilled leaders with all the right attributes and experiences will sometimes fail due to factors beyond their control. These elements are external environmental factors which vary from industry to industry. For example, a housing market crash can affect a leader's success if that leader is working in the mortgage industry.

3.11 THE NORTHHOUSE APPROACH

Northhouse brings the Katz and Mumford theories together in a three-skills approach: **administrative skills**, **interpersonal skills**, and **conceptual skills.** Each of these has, contained within it, subsets of skills. Northhouse believes that the Katz three-skills approach and the Mumford three-competencies approach can be organized together for a better picture of leadership skills. See figure 3.1.

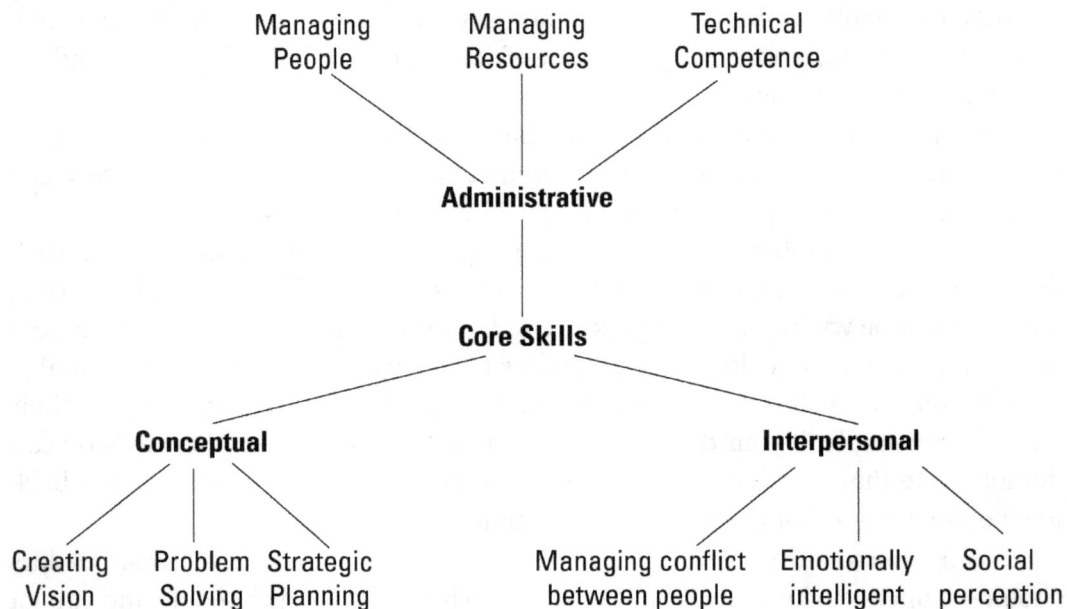

Figure 3.2: The Three-Skills Approach
Source: Original Work
Attribution: Heather Mbaye
License: CC BY-SA 4.0

3.11.1 Administrative Skills

According to Northhouse, good leadership is founded upon administrative skills. These are the basic skills that all leaders must have and include managing people, managing resources, and having technical competence.

Skills in managing people have two dimensions. Leaders must manage the technical side of supervising workers, meaning that they must oversee, understand, and evaluate the actual work being done. Leaders must also focus on the social side of managing employees, which means understanding people, helping people feel competent, and grasping the social environment. This focus can often prove to be the most time-consuming aspect of management. Creating a team and maintaining that team feeling, employee motivation, and the promoting of good relations between people all take time. In an office setting, for example, a good department manager doesn't just sit in their office. They take a moment a couple of times a day to go around to the offices of their faculty and chat with each one, letting them know that their manager is interested while also giving them the opportunity to express both positive and negative aspects of their jobs. Additionally, effective leaders must play an active role in searching out and retaining productive and skilled employees.

According to Northhouse, another aspect of administrative skill is understanding how to manage resources. Resources include skilled employees, cashflow, office or production space, supplies and equipment, raw materials, and anything else needed to accomplish the organization's goals. A good leader must manage the acquisition of new resources, allocate those which they already have, and sometimes re-structure that allocation in the light of new goals or new employees. A leader who mismanages resources, or whose subordinates do, will not continue as a leader for long.

As with Katz's theory, Northhouse considers technical competence as necessary specialized knowledge, which makes it the third component of the administrative skill set. Without technical competence and industry knowledge, a leader cannot succeed. Still, technical competence can be learned if a leader has the motivation and capacity to learn, develop, and study. In addition to specialized industry knowledge, a leader must be familiar with the legal requirements of employing people from a human resources perspective, including familiarity with sexual harassment laws, legal requirements for documenting employee issues, and the requirements for interviewing new applicants(that is, knowing the questions you are not allowed to ask). A leader who ignores the legal requirements of the country in which they work will not long be in a management position.

3.11.2 Interpersonal Skills

The second core skill set presented by Northhouse is interpersonal. These abilities are the people skills that allow good leaders to effectively work with their colleagues. Such social skills include social perceptiveness, emotional intelligence, and conflict management.

The social perceptiveness subset of skills includes most of the "people" skills with which we may be most familiar, and yet sometimes have difficulty defining. Managers must understand that not everyone is the same; each person has their own ideas about what's important and necessary. People are motivated by a myriad of different factors. Everyone responds differently to stimuli, and every team needs a different combination of elements in order to be successful. When working to become more effective in creating the most efficient outcomes for their team, leaders must develop a fairly good idea of how a person or group of people will respond to change and new challenges.

Emotional intelligence, the second subset of interpersonal skills, entails being able to understand one's own emotions while also grasping that others will have different emotions. Leaders must manage their own emotional response when facing the emotional responses of others: "Specifically, emotional intelligence can be defined as the ability to perceive and express emotions, to use emotions to facilitate thinking, to understand and reason with emotions, and to manage emotions effectively within oneself and in relationships with others" (Northhouse, 2012, p. 91). Leaders must be aware of their own emotions and their causes in order to communicate clearly and help others successfully. Second, leaders need to be aware of other people's emotions and try to understand those emotions' source(s). Leaders should exhibit empathy towards others, so listening is key. Keeping in mind that it is nearly impossible to entirely divorce emotions from decision making, leaders must understand and channel those emotions productively.

Conflict is inescapable. It's going to happen in any team and organization. When leaders are adept at conflict management, the third subset of Mumford's skills, they can ease the issues surrounding a problem. Such conflicts are complex and can be difficult to address, but a good leader will take on conflict and even use it to innovate and improve team morale and performance. Chapter 6 focuses on conflict management.

3.11.3 Conceptual Skills

Conceptual skills, the third group of core skills set forth by Northhouse, are those visionary skills also discussed by Katz, Mumford, and his colleagues. These skills include problem solving, strategic planning, and vision creation.

Some people are natural problem solvers. They see a problem and right away start thinking about how to fix it, but problem solving is a skill that can also be learned. Effective leaders will eventually discover that they must apply their knowledge and experience to problems that arise on a daily basis. Although experience is an excellent guide, leaders should be aware that not every similar problem will have the same solution. It's important to be able to "think outside the box," too, to craft individual and innovative solutions for an organization's difficulties.

According to Northhouse, it's important first to identify the problem properly and early. Not everyone sees problems, and some people fail to place importance on issues when they are seen. Some people will refuse to believe something is a problem until it blows up; even then, they may downplay the situation. Some problems are simple and obvious; others appear simple but aren't; and many are complex and difficult. Second, he says, leaders should generate alternate solutions. They may complete this process themselves or bring in key actors for a brainstorming session. Third, leaders and team members will select the best solution and implement their chosen strategy until the problem is solved.

Strategic planning as a subset of conceptual skills; it involves setting major goals for an organization and thinking purposefully about how to deploy people and resources to achieve the chosen objectives. Some organizations, like universities, have strategic plans in which they do just that. More specifically, strategic planning involves goal setting, followed by creating a series of short, medium, and long-term plans to achieve those goals. Strategic leaders do not, however, slavishly follow the plan; they are flexible and adaptable to changing circumstances.

Visionary leaders see a future that is brighter than the present. They must see goals and tasks on the way to that future; they must communicate that vision to others and convince everyone to "get on board" and realize that vision for the organization. Chapter 4 discusses visionary skills further.

A good leader balances all of these many skills. However, most people don't possess every skill in equal measure. Some leaders are better at managing people through emotional perception, some at creating vision, and still others at managing resources.

Northhouse brings together the skills theories we have discussed in this chapter. However, it is up to a manager to balance all of these skills and recognize any deficiencies they may have. It is possible to gain skills, to learn skills in order to become a better leader. However, each leader should practice reflection to determine how to best balance the skills needed with the skills they already have.

Leadership in Action

Ibrahim is a District Vice President for a large retail company. He manages a team of employees that, in turn, each manage a store in the chain. He doesn't see the team every day because the stores are spread out over a large geographic area. Instead, the team meets once per quarter (4 times per year), each time rotating the store in which the meeting takes place.

Generally, Ibrahim emails directions that contain action plans and sales goals; he also visits each store on a regular basis to meet with the teams there. This strategy works pretty well for most of his employees, but Sonia, one of his longest running managers, has been "checking out" recently. She has always been trustworthy and a good employee who meets all her goals, so Ibrahim hasn't needed to check in with her as often. While she used to exceed all the sales goals that were set, her store is now just reaching the minimums.

Ibrahim does some research and realizes that he's missed her store in the regular visit rotations and hasn't really communicated with her at all, except in his group emails. Even at the last two quarterly meetings, he didn't have a chance to check in with her on an individual basis.

He realizes that he needs to get in touch, so he calls her. Instead of recriminations, he apologizes for failing to check in and asks how she is doing.

It turns out that Sonia wants more challenges at work than her store manager job offers. Ibrahim discovers that Sonia has recently finished her Master of Business Administration, so he suggests that Sonia apply for the regional financial manager position that is about to open up.

After this discussion, Ibrahim found that Sonia's work habits returned to their previous levels. He used social leadership skills to communicate with her and figure out her needs, and task leadership to find a new position for her that would best use her strengths to help accomplish the company's goals.

3.12 SUMMARY

Leadership styles vary from task-oriented to social-oriented and everywhere in between. Task-oriented individuals need to be: creating structure, making lists, and distributing workloads. Social leaders need to be connected to their teams: creating relationships, making group decisions, and distributing praise. The best leaders will use their social leadership skills to support their teams in reaching their goals, goals they created and pursue with task management skills in mind. Good managers, in other words, will be both task oriented and social oriented leaders.

Furthermore, this chapter presents three theories on the skill sets that leaders should have, develop, and/or learn in order to be most effective. Contrary to earlier studies of leaders, which discussed leadership "traits" as if leaders were born rather than made, the approaches in this chapter show that leaders can apply themselves to learn certain skills. Not everyone will be equally successful or experienced in all areas. In fact, different types of leaders need different mixes of skills. It's not necessary to create vision when you are a shift manager in a store, but interpersonal skills and technical knowledge would be critical. Vice presidents may not need to know the technical aspects of running an assembly line; instead, they need to manage production workloads and resources. The three theories discussed present the many invaluable skills needed for effective leadership, some unique, some with overlap. But the bottom line with all of the theories is that these skills may be learned over time and with experience. Effective leaders can be made.

In the next chapter, we turn to missions, visions, and plans. All leaders ultimately should contribute to the mission of the organization, to its vision and its strategic plan. Leaders should be instrumental in creating missions, visions, and plans, but they must also contribute to the successful implementation of these designs. The next chapter surveys organizational and leadership values while examining how leaders are confined to work within these areas.

3.13 DISCUSSION QUESTIONS

1. If you had to choose, would you say you are a more task-oriented or social-oriented leader?

2. If you had to choose, would you prefer to follow a task-oriented or social-oriented leader? Why?

3. What are the most important aspects of each type of leader?

4. What is the best combination of skills for task and social leaders?

5. What is the most important skill in Katz's Three-Skill model?

6. What kinds of environmental factors can prevent a good leader from being successful?

7. How can managing resources create challenges that conflict management skills can help address?

8. Which of the skills in the chapter would you say you need to work on most?

9. Which of the skills in the chapter do you exhibit, to some degree, already?

3.14 FURTHER READING

3 Leadership Stories to Help You Be A Better Manager https://getlighthouse.com/blog/leadership-stories-help-better-manager/

Bris, Arturo 2019. What is really eating Apple – and why Steve Jobs would not be doing a lot better. http://theconversation.com/what-is-really-eating-apple-and-why-steve-jobs-would-not-be-doing-a-lot-better-109377

Five Lessons from a Bad Boss. https://www.forbes.com/sites/dedehenley/2018/04/23/five-lessons-from-a-bad-boss/#1143fe9c71f2

Katz, R. L. (1974, September/October). Skills of an effective administrator, Harvard Business Review, 52(5), 90–102. https://hbr.org/1974/09/skills-of-an-effective-administrator

Raise Your Game: Relationship-Oriented vs Task-Oriented At The Workplace (podcast) https://leaderonomics.com/leadership/ryg-relationship-vs-task-oriented

3.15 RESOURCES

Bandura, Comille Tapiwa, Maria Kavussanu, and Chin Wei Ong. 2019. "Authentic Leadership and Task Cohesion: The Mediating Role of Trust and Team Sacrifice." Group Dynamics: Theory, Research, and Practice, August 26, 2019.

Katz, R. L. (1974, September/October). Skills of an effective administrator, Harvard Business Review, 52(5), 90–102.

Kimmorly, S. (2017). Gail Kelly on what it means to be a successful modern leader. Business Insider Australia. April 21, 2017. Accessed September 2020. https://www.businessinsider.com.au/gail-kelly-on-what-it-means-to-be-a-successful-modern-leader-2017-4.

Leonard, Karen Moustafa, and Fatma Pakdil. 2016. Performance Leadership. Human Resource Management and Organizational Behavior Collection.

Martin, Ann M. 2013. Empowering Leadership: Developing Behaviors for Success. Chicago, Ill: AASL.

Mikkelson, Alan C., David Sloan, and Colin Hesse. 2019. "Relational Communication Messages and Leadership Styles in Supervisor/Employee Relationships." International Journal of Business Communication 56 (4): 586–604.

Mumford, M. D., Zaccaro, S. J., Connelly, M. S., & Marks, M. A. (2000). Leadership skills: Conclusions and future directions. The Leadership Quarterly, 11(1), 155–170.

Mumford, M. D., Zaccaro, S. J., Harding, F. D., Jacobs, T., & Fleishman, E. A. (2000). Leadership skills for a changing world: Solving complex problems. The Leadership Quarterly, 11(1), 11–35.

Northouse, P. G. (2012). Introduction to Leadership: concepts and practice (2nd ed.). Thousand Oaks, CA: Sage.

Olson, David T. Discovering Your Leadership Style: The Power of Chemistry, Strategy and Spirituality. IVP Books, 2014.

Rees, James and Stephen J. Spignesi. 2011. George Washington's Leadership Lessons: What the Father of Our Country Can Teach Us About Effective Leadership and Character. John Wiley & Sons, 2011.

Zaccaro, S. J., Mumford, M. D., Connelly, M. S., Marks, M. A., & Gilbert, J. A. (2000). Assessment of leader problem-solving capabilities. The Leadership Quarterly, 11(1), 37–64.

4 Creating a Vision

4.1 LEARNING OBJECTIVES

After reading this chapter students will
1. Understand the critical components of a vision
2. Recognize methods that will aid in building consensus around shared ideas
3. Be able to apply techniques to assess the effectiveness of a vision

4.2 KEY TERMS

- Mission Statement
- Transformational Leadership
- Charismatic Leadership
- Vision Statement
- Consensus building
- Implementation
- Evaluation
- Organizational Culture
- Organizational Values
- SWOT Matrix

4.3 INTRODUCTION

In the previous chapter, we discussed the various styles of leadership and the characteristics that these leaders embody. In addition, you were introduced to skillsets that the most successful leaders develop and nurture in order to become more effective. However, regardless of the particular leadership style and skillsets a leader chooses to develop, effective leadership within an organization also requires that the organization knows where they want to go and understands what it takes to get there. In order to clearly articulate this destination, organizations create vision statements. It is easy to confuse **mission statements** and **vision statements**. A mission statement articulates what it is that the organization is currently doing or accomplishing. Mission statements tend to be action oriented and clarify what an organization does. Mission statements also tend to be consistent and relatively static, largely because the ongoing purpose of an organization tends to remain constant over time. Mission statements usually contain the following characteristics:

- **They are Short:** Mission statements are short so that they are memorable and easy for people to remember.

- **They are Specific:** Mission statements highlight what makes a company different from other organizations that perform similar functions.

- **They are Realistic:** Mission statements are about what is happening now, not what an organization would like to see happen.

- **They are Action Based:** Mission statements tell you what a company does. They should explain the "what" of an organization.

Let's examine a few mission statements from some very innovative organizations. Pay close attention to how these mission statements incorporate the characteristics listed above.

4.3.1 Evaluating Mission Statements

JetBlue: "To inspire humanity–both in the air and on the ground"

- JetBlue's mission is an interesting one, as it does not necessarily make immediately apparent what the company does. Rather, this mission focuses on how they intend to accomplish their intended goal. Their mission statement is realistic—it highlights what the experience will be like—it is short—one sentence is easy to remember and recite—and it is specific to this company—more accurately, it is specific when compared to other airline mission statements. Overall, this is an effective and unique mission statement.

TED: "Spread ideas"

- TED's mission statement seems almost ridiculously simple, but it encapsulates exactly what TED aims to do through its free inspirational talks. The talks are intended to make you think, and this mission statement checks all of the boxes for an effective mission statement. It is short, specific, explains exactly what the company does, and is realistic. This is an excellent mission statement.

LinkedIn: "To connect the world's professionals to make them more productive and successful."

- LinkedIn is very explicit in explaining what they want to do. Their goal is to connect professionals in a way that allows them to be more successful. Remarkably, that is exactly what they do. Leaders from all over the world are able to connect with each other, share resumes and offer advice and inspiration to one another regardless of their location.

Amazon: "To be Earth's most customer-centric company, where customers can find and discover anything they might want to buy online, and endeavors to offer its customers the lowest possible prices."

- No company is likely more ubiquitous in the online shopping world than Amazon. It is known for its ability to connect its customers with any product they can think of at affordable prices and with remarkably fast shipping. They are known for their customer service and generous return policy. It certainly seems that Amazon lives up to its mission.

A vision statement, on the other hand, offers a more aspirational idea that highlights what it is that the company hopes to be in the future. Vision statements often help organizations to align their philosophy, mission, and actions.

In this chapter, we will examine organizational vision and the theory that underlies it. We will define organizational vision and focus on how organizational values and mission inform the vision. We will also discuss how a leader builds consensus around their vision. The chapter will conclude with an exploration of effective practices for implementing a vision, including the challenges surrounding the assessment and reevaluation of a vision.

4.4 CREATING A VISION: A PRIMER

We are going to examine the literature and theories that undergird the necessity of having a coherent and powerful vision. These approaches will offer us both a theoretical and practical framework from which to approach creating, implementing, and assessing your organizational vision.

4.4.1 The Leadership Literature: An Overview

Franklin Covey Company, widely regarded as one of the premiere leadership consulting companies in the world, lays out the four essential roles of leadership. One of the four key roles Covey identifies is the need to convey a clear vision. The Covey company leadership framework notes that having a clear vision requires individuals to be adept change agents because vision involves change. This requirement is broadened into a larger organizational context, where the organization examines its mission, vision, and strategy. Note that for our purposes, a mission is the purpose of an organization, vision is the direction for the organization, and strategy is laying out the path for achieving organizational success. All of these ideas work in concert with one another, but the most critical component of this process is that the organization is aware of the direction in which it is moving.

Loehr and Schwartz (2011), in their work *The Power of Full Engagement*, note that people are mission-specific, their primary goal being to mobilize their sources of energy in order to accomplish an intended undertaking (and that mission/goal can be personal or professional). People in an organization want to be connected to a clearly articulated mission and vision and are likely to embrace that goal and work to achieve it.

Similarly, Kouzes and Posner, in their five practices of exemplary leadership, offer that creating and sharing a vision is critical to truly effective leadership. They note that effective leaders believe they have the ability to make a difference. As such, they have the skill and ability to paint a picture of the future that compels people to believe in what the organization can become (as opposed to simply what it currently is). Kouzes and Posner assert that effective leaders are experts in persuasion who are able to convince others to follow their vision. In other words, not only do these individuals have a vision, but they also have significant skill at getting others to join in achieving that vision through inspiring action. The most effective leaders recognize the potential in an organization (or individual) and then build consensus around a vision of what the organization can be.

4.4.2 The Importance of Vision

As discussed in chapter 1, **transformational leadership** (a term coined by James MacGregor Burns in 1978) is a theory of leadership in which a leader works with a team to identify an area (or areas) of change within an organization. With this concept, the leader helps to shape a vision that will aid in guiding the organization through targeted change that addresses critical issues within the organization. The leader is focused on motivating and inspiring the members of the organization because they believe increased morale will result in increased productivity. These leaders also have tremendous abilities to adapt to changing conditions and situations, which allows individuals to perform at levels exceeding their own personal capabilities. Odumeru and Ogbonna (2013) note that "transformational leadership inspires people to achieve unexpected or remarkable results. It gives workers autonomy over specific jobs, as well as the authority to make decisions once they have been trained." These leaders are so important because they are able to elevate an organization beyond what the organization is to what it can be.

Charismatic Leadership, discussed in chapter 2, suggests that effective leadership is based not upon formal titles but on the characteristics of a leader and their ability to bring about substantial and significant change (Weber, 1966). The primary characteristic of the charismatic leader is, of course, charisma, meaning the ability to influence or persuade people to engage in particular sets of behaviors that lead to, in this instance, organizational success.

As a characteristic, however, charisma can be a bit nebulous. Max Weber (1966) noted that "the term 'charisma' will be applied to a certain quality of individual personality by virtue of which he is set apart from ordinary men and treated as endowed with supernatural, superhuman, or at least specifically exceptional powers or qualities." Though in practice the term is not quite so otherworldly, charisma is still difficult to quantify or operationalize.

Charisma at its heart is about the emotional impact a leader has on their followers, based largely on the personal characteristics of that leader. House and Shamir (1993) integrate various theories on charismatic leadership and offer this summary of shared qualities and abilities of charismatic leaders:

- Vision

- Ability to motivate followers

- Excellent role modeling

- A positive self-image

- Ability to empower followers

The most important characteristics are the abilities to articulate a vision and to find ways to motivate and empower followers toward that idea. Regardless of the type of vision exhibited by the leader, the steps to formulating an effective vision follow a common path.

Each of these theories illustrate the importance of understanding who you are as an organization and who you are as a leader in order to inspire others to work towards a collective goal. People are driven by goals and structure, and your organizational vision provides a roadmap for your employees to follow in order to achieve success.

4.5 STEPS TO BUILDING A VISION

Leaders need more than simply having an idea of what their organization is about. Leaders must be able to clearly articulate and communicate that message to stakeholders both inside and outside of their organization. Regardless of what "leadership camp" you subscribe to, you must be able to convince people that you know where you are going and that it is worthwhile for them to follow you.

4.5.1 Step One: Articulating a Vision

In order to lead people capably, you need to be able to convince people that you are moving in the right direction. That is, articulating your vision is a critically important component of having vision. It is not enough to simply have a vision; you have to be able to take the vision and communicate it in a succinct, understandable, and inspiring way in order to convince people to follow you. Alan Mulally, former President and CEO of Ford Motor Company, said, "It's important to have a compelling vision and a comprehensive plan. Positive leadership–

conveying the idea that there is always a way forward—is so important because that is what you are here for—to figure out how to move the organization forward [sic]." Articulation of a vision is about showing people the way forward. Watch this video of Simon Sinek arguing that "a leader without a vision is a follower."

https://www.youtube.com/watch?v=K6fAKWHdWHg

Here are some tips on articulating a vision within an organization:

1. **The message should be simple:** Your vision should be clear and concise. Albert Einstein is credited with saying, "if you can't explain it simply, you don't understand it well enough." You need to be able to articulate your vision to varied audiences in ways that they can understand and implement. It should be clear when people hear your vision that they know what your company does and what your company is about.

2. **Tailor your message to fit your audience:** When communicating your message, it needs to be easily understood by all constituents, both within and outside the organization. This requirement means that the way you talk about your vision may change depending on your audience. The central tenant of your vision should not change, but the way you deliver the message should change. For people outside of your organization, this concept may mean eliminating jargon or insider language. For the Board of Directors, you need to focus on the bottom line. In effect, your audience should dictate the style and tone you use when you talk about your vision.

3. **Repeat your vision until you live your vision:** Your vision should be an ingrained part of your company's fabric and how it operates. Your vision should be the driving factor behind the decision-making processes related to your organization. Everyone within the organization should have a sense of what you are about and where the organization is headed—remember, they might not say it in exactly the same way, but your message should still be clear. So, repeat your vision, constantly.

4.5.2 Step Two: Building Consensus Around a Vision

Once you have shared your vision both inside and outside the organization, you need to gain the all-important buy-in for your vision. **Consensus building** comprises the process by which conflict is mediated to achieve agreement. In order to build consensus behind a vision, it is critical to identify all interested parties, bring them on board, and build trust between them. Remember that consensus does not mean unanimous agreement; rather, it means there is overwhelming agreement between all critical stakeholders within an organization which has been achieved through good faith efforts.

Consensus can be difficult to gain for several reasons:[1]

- **Your stakeholders are not hearing each other:** They have either not heard or understood the other points of view. They do not fully understand the vision.

- **Your stakeholders have different values or experiences:** Your constituents understand one another, but they simply do not hold the same value sets and structures. They don't think the vision supports their values.

- **Your stakeholders are affected by outside factors:** Some external factors, unrelated to the task at hand, affect the way that your team members think about and act towards one another. External factors affect the way they perceive the vision.

Most challenges to build consensus stem from the first obstacle. When people do not fully understand the vision, they have a difficult time embracing it so they can't necessarily determine their place in pursuing it. Inspiring leaders lay out a roadmap that details the what and the why. This roadmap to consensus includes the following:

- **Be clear:** Your organizational vision lays out exactly where your organization is going. Simon Sinek, author and motivational speaker, notes, "Vision is a destination, a fixed point to which we focus all effort. Strategy is a route, an adaptable path to get us where we want to go." People have to know where they are heading; otherwise, you risk losing the commitment and buy-in of your team members.

- **Be Audacious:** William Huthinson Murray wrote, "boldness has genius, and magic and power in it." The vision you articulate needs to be compelling. Your vision needs to inspire people on an individual level. Though the vision clearly articulates where the organization is heading, the individuals who are part of your organization need to determine how the vision applies to them specifically. One of your primary tasks, then, is to make the vision "come to life." You need to show people how they can contribute to, and benefit from, the larger mission and vision of the organization. Remember that when people own something, they tend to take better care of it. When the members of your team own the vision, they are much more likely to commit to it and ultimately help the organization achieve it.

- **Communicate Purpose:** While it is critical that people understand the "how" of your vision, they need also to understand its "why." To truly gain consensus, people have to understand the purpose of your

---

1   https://www.leadstrat.com/the-art-of-getting-to-yes-5-techniques-for-building-consensus-2/, accessed 12/21/19

vision, and your vision has to have purpose. Why should they be motivated to pursue this mission? As Henry David Thoreau wrote in *Walden Pond*, "It's not enough to be busy, so are the ants. The question is, what are we busy about?" Leaders need to remember that purpose is different for different individuals and constituents. Though for you as the leader the purpose of your vision might be to increase productivity on your sales team, the members of the sales team may have a different purpose through your vision. For example, their individual purpose may be to earn a promotion and thereby a better life for their family. If you communicate your purpose clearly, members of your organization are able to determine how they can make that purpose work for them.

4.5.3 Step Three: Implementing a Vision

A good plan and buy-in will only get you so far: the real challenge posed by having a vision is making it happen. **Implementation** comprises the process of putting a decision or plan into place. After convincing people to embrace your vision, you next need to convince them to take the steps needed to turn it into a reality. Accountability is key in these steps. Employees need to know exactly what they are expected to do as well as the consequences to themselves and the organization if they do not compete their tasks. Erica Olsen notes, "Implementation is the process that turns strategies and plans into actions in order to accomplish strategic objectives and goals."[2] Here are some key steps to implementation:

- **Establish Your Priorities:** It is easy to get sidetracked. Your vision is likely to have several tangentially connected areas that you could focus on. A good vision, though, does not try to do everything or be everything to all people. Rather, it focuses on the specific priorities you laid out within your vision statement. All implementation actions you take should directly relate to the achievement of your goals. You need to prioritize actions that address the most critical issues and challenges facing your organization. These priorities should be directly tied to your **organizational values** and your **organizational culture.** Again, organizational values are the ideas and principles that guide organizational actions. Organizational culture describes the way people behave within the organization. The implementation of your vision must directly connect with both culture and values in order to be successful.

- **Develop Action Plans with Accountability Structures Built In:** The implementation must have actionable items. This idea means that every single piece of the implementation plan can be measured and assessed. The expectations of members within your organization needs to be definable, concrete, and clear. As a general rule, the action

---

2   https://onstrategyhq.com/resources/strategic-implementation/, accessed December 22, 2019

plan you create in order to implement your vision should have a discrete timetable, and the action plan should be directly tied to your organizational mission and vision. In other words, you should not allow yourself to be distracted by factors that don't help you achieve your goals. In addition, accountability structures must be built into your implementation plan so that you are able to track your progress to see if you are moving towards making your vision a reality.

- **Identify Potential Pitfalls:** To implement the plan and achieve the vision, effective leaders must first determine what obstacles could stand in the way. Risk is an unavoidable component of organizational change; however, mitigating risk is the best way to ensure success. Effective leaders don't just have a "Plan A." They also have **contingency plans** set up in the event that their original plan doesn't go exactly as anticipated. The purpose of a contingency plan is to ensure that your company can operate effectively in the event of an unforeseen circumstance. Contingency plans allow you to "hope for the best but prepare for the worst." They thereby allow companies to be more flexible so they can adjust to any unforeseen events that may transpire in the future. Contingency plans also send a message to those within the organization that your company is a forward-thinking entity ready to deal with potential challenges and market shifts. Importantly, contingency plans are not only useful in planning for potential disasters, but they also help to mitigate the challenges of losing a key employee, for instance. Having a quality contingency plan helps organizations stay on the path to achieving their organizational aims and goals.

Let's look at a few really effective vision statements. Notice that these vision statements incorporate many of the characteristics we have already mentioned in this chapter. Remember that the most effective vision statements are simple, a bit audacious, and are tailored to a specific audience.

4.5.4 Effective Vision Statements

Disney: "To entertain, inform and inspire people around the globe with unparalleled storytelling, reflecting the iconic brands, creative minds and innovative technologies that make ours the world's premier entertainment company."

- Disney does not waste any time in letting us know that they plan on being the best entertainment company in the world and that they will do so through their ability to tell innovative stories. Most would agree that Disney lives this vision every single day through their immersive theme parks and some of the most iconic films of all time. This vision statement is extremely effective because these ideas are certainly synonymous with Disney—to the point that when we hear that Disney is making a new movie or opening a new theme park, we simply expect it to be innovative and trendsetting.

Warby Parker: "To offer designer eyewear at a revolutionary price, while leading the way for socially conscious business."
- Warby Parker is a newer company, but one that makes it very clear their business is eyewear and that *what* they do is equally important to *how* they do it. Their commitment to social consciousness sets them apart from other companies. Essentially, they are telling their customers that they can buy glasses elsewhere; however, if they care about the environment and the world around them, they should purchase eyewear from Warby Parker. In addition, they use language that is intentionally evocative. Offering their eyewear at a revolutionary price implies they are willing to upset the market to commit to their goal. Their audacity sets them apart in a crowded field.

IKEA: "To create a better everyday life for the many people."
- IKEA's vision is very similar to the company itself: it's simple but effective. Their vision is not about the products they sell but about the way that they want their products to impact people. Their vision sells customers on the idea that their furniture is accessible. They are trying to make life better for as many people as possible, which also implies that their products are likely very affordable. It's an extremely simple but effective vision statement.

4.5.5 Assessing a Vision

After you have implemented your vision, the next step is to assess your vision. A clear plan should be in place for gathering and then evaluating information in order to determine if the organization has achieved its vision and if that vision was the right one. In other words, a plan should be in place to collect data to enable an organization to measure the achievement and attainment of specifically stated goalposts.

Information Gathering

Assessment always begins with information gathering. You need to know exactly what your organization is achieving (key benchmarks and metrics). You need to figure out how your people are feeling—about their jobs, about the organization, about your leadership. Many information gathering tools can be utilized to aid in the assessment of your vision:
- **Questionnaires and Surveys:** These materials offer a good way to gather a lot of surface level data from a large group of people.
- **Personal Interviews:** Talking to people in the organization is a great way to gather information regarding how the changes and the change

process are affecting the actual people who make up the organization. They can include things like focus groups and targeted one-on-one interviews.

- **Deep Dive into the Data:** Looking at the numbers can give you a good look into trends and patterns that can provide valuable information on whether the organization achieved the vision and whether the vision was the right one for the organization. This information should be both quantitative data (financials, revenue projections) and qualitative data (customer feedback, internal satisfaction surveys). These particulars can include document reviews, organizational observations, and case studies.

The key to information gathering is varying the information gathering tools to best fit the organizational mission and values and to collate the best intel on how the organization was affected by the change.

Evaluation

After information gathering, the assessment enters the **evaluation** phase. In the evaluation phase, you try to determine what all of the information you have gathered actually means. A good rule of thumb by which to evaluate is to conduct a S.W.O.T. analysis, as displayed in figure 4.1. A S.W.O.T. analysis is a strategic planning technique that helps an organization identify its strengths, weaknesses, opportunities, and threats, usually related to a specific project. A S.W.O.T. analysis can be extremely useful in determining how and if a vision is positioning an organization for success.

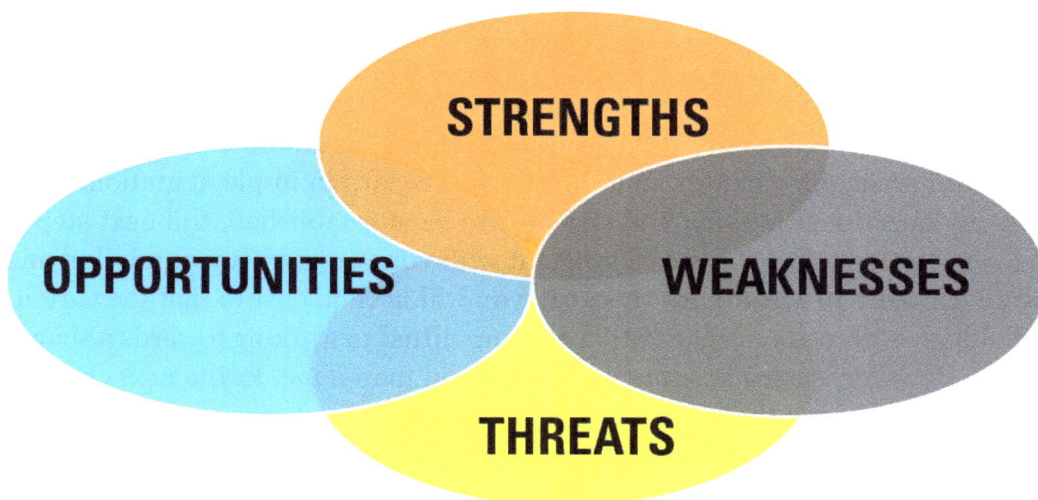

Figure 4.1: A S.W.O.T. Analysis Matrix
Source: Original Work
Attribution: Matthew Hipps
License: CC BY-SA 4.0

Understanding a S.W.O.T. analysis requires a strong comprehension of each individual evaluative area within the matrix. **Strengths** are an internal factor describing the organization's characteristics that lead to success. These characteristics can be actual, like the size of the workforce, or abstract, like the organizational culture or reputation. **Weaknesses** are also governed by internal factors and are characteristics that inhibit the organization's success. These elements can also be actual or abstract. **Opportunities** are generally governed by external factors; opportunities are any conditions, situations, or factors that can help lead to organizational growth. In a S.W.O.T. analysis, we are assuming that growth is the primary goal of any organization (defined in ways that are specific to a particular organization). **Threats** are also governed by external factors; threats pose a risk to the organization's success. Threats are always negative and never advance the organization's goals. Such threats could include market conditions, a shrinking customer base, overall demographics, etc.

S.W.O.T. is a good analytical tool because it requires that you analyze all aspects of your organization to determine if your organization's reality (its strengths, weaknesses, and opportunities) is aligned with what it's actually trying to accomplish. Simply listing these characteristics is not enough. There must be a critical analysis of how these factors can help shape the organizational vision— and how that vision can be used to help transform the organization's mission and actions. Good leaders will not shy away from this evaluation; rather, they welcome it, knowing that it is the only way to improve and thus achieve goals in a more effective manner.

4.6 SUMMARY

A vision is central to a successful organization. Yet having an organizational vision is not enough; an effective leader must clearly articulate the vision, inspire employees to embrace it, implement steps to achieve it, and evaluate (and adjust) the company's progress towards measurable goals. Evaluation should be continual and intentional, allowing for adjustments and tweaks in implementation. Once your organizational mission and vision have been established, the next step is to lead your team in a manner consistent with your organizational mission and vision. In order to accomplish this goal, you will have to ensure that the various individuals within your organization are committed to working towards a shared vision. However, such a statement is easier said than done. In the next chapter, we will explore how the most effective leaders are able to bring diverse teams together and foster inclusivity within their organizations. The next chapter will also walk you through the process of building a sustained culture of inclusivity, illustrating ways in which you can turn the differences found within your organization into assets.

4.7 DISCUSSION QUESTIONS

1. How important is vision in your current or intended career? How does (or would) it affect your performance as a leader?

2. How does one develop a vision?

3. Can people work towards conflicting visions and goals and still be effective? Why or why not?

4. Why are people so resistant to change? What helps overcome this resistance?

5. Explaining your vision to others is a key part of effective leadership, yet there is often skepticism when someone proposes risking change. How does a leader overcome this skepticism?

4.8 REFERENCES

Bass, Bernard M. (1990). "From transactional to transformational leadership: Learning to share the vision". *Organizational Dynamics*. **18** (3): 19–31. doi:10.1016/0090-2616(90)90061-S.

https://www.ckju.net/en/dossier/how-charismatic-leaders-gain-commitment-their-vision-and-mission-organization.

https://www.leadstrat.com/the-art-of-getting-to-yes-5-techniques-for-building-consensus-2/, accessed December 2019.

https://magazine.vunela.com/4-steps-to-creating-a-shared-vision-that-will-energize-your-team-82b801e742ed, accessed 12/21/19.

https://www.amanet.org/articles/transforming-vision-into-reality/.

https://www.creativejeffrey.com/creative/implement.php.

https://thethrivingsmallbusiness.com/implementing-business-strategy/.

http://literacybasics.ca/strategic-planning/strategic-planning-assessment/.

https://www.shrm.org/resourcesandtools/tools-and-samples/toolkits/pages/understandinganddevelopingorganizationalculture.aspx.

https://vc.franklincovey.com/tc/public/workbooks/LEA170788_Create%20Shared%20Vision%20Strategy_Mod_v1.3.5_HRE_preview.pdf.

http://www.leadershipchallenge.com/About-section-Our-Approach.aspx.

https://blog.hubspot.com/marketing/inspiring-company-mission-statements.

Odumeru, J. A., & Ogbonna, I. G. (2013). Transformational vs. transactional leadership theories: Evidence in literature. International Review of Management and Business Research, 2(2), 355.

"Transformational Leadership". Business Dictionary. Retrieved 2016-05-23.

5 Leadership in a Diverse and Inclusive Organization

5.1 LEARNING OBJECTIVES

After reading this chapter students will

1. Define organizational diversity and inclusion

2. Explore a brief social history of how these concepts have become significant in the current organizational culture

3. Understand various leadership strategies, approaches, and techniques that apply to this leadership challenge

4. Use various leadership examples and practical applications to understand how organizational diversity and inclusion can be achieved

5.2 KEY TERMS

- Diversity
- Inclusion
- Adaptive work
- Group-identity
- In-group/out-group

5.3 INTRODUCTION

This chapter will address leadership in a diverse and inclusive organizational environment. Chapter one defines leadership as "the action of leading a group of people or an organization" (Oxford University). The challenge explored in this chapter is leading an organization to embrace a culture of inclusiveness. The chapter will trace the history of **diversity** and inclusiveness in organizations and how leadership theory has embraced these new trends through applying adaptive work, managing **out-groups**, discovering a personal mission, and addressing inclusive personal traits.

5.4 DIVERSITY AND INCLUSIVENESS

Diversity's definition is quite simple: "the condition or fact of being different or varied; variety." The definition of inclusiveness is a little more complex: "the quality of including many different types of people and treating them all fairly and equally" (Cambridge Dictionary). For purposes of this chapter, we will use a more current and targeted description of the two terms. Jim Turley, Former Chairman and CEO of Ernst and Young and the current Director of Citibank, draws a distinction between the two: "Diversity itself is about the mix of people you have, and creating an inclusive culture is about making that mix work" (Groysberg and Connolly, 2014).

Ajay Banga, MasterCard CEO

My passion for diversity comes from the fact that I myself am diverse. There have been a hundred times when I have felt different from other people in the room or in the business. I have a turban and a full beard, and I run a global company—that's not common.

5.5 DIVERSITY

Using Turley's definition, we see that the term diversity represents the composition of people within an organization. Diversity made its way into organizations from a legal perspective in 1964 with the passage of the Title VII Civil Rights Act. Title VII had a significant impact on organizations and their leadership. The act dictated that certain groups of people had to be provided a greater opportunity and equal access to careers within all organizations. These groups included racial, gender, religious, and cultural groups. As time progressed, Title VII has been amended to include many other different types of groups as well, which incorporate sexual orientation, age, and disabilities (Dishman, 2018).

In many ways, the concept of diversity in organizations has evolved from purely legal compliance to a social justice focus, to a personal awareness and acceptance. Nevertheless, the concept of diversity and the positive attributes of diversity have still a long way to go in reaching their full importance within many organizations. A 2015 study from Deloitte's Leadership Initiative indicated that generational shifts may re-define the meaning and significance of diversity. The study found that Boomers (born 1946 to1964) and Gen. Xers (born 1965 to 1979) saw diversity as a fairness process that focused on protecting members of specific groups. However, Millennials (born 1980 to 2000) defined diversity as a mixing of different backgrounds and individual perspectives, including the more subtle notion of out-groups. These findings indicate that not only is the cultural understanding of diversity changing, but also the concept/ identification of diversity has become an accepted social norm (Dishman, 2015).

As mentioned above, this newer classification occurring in literature is the formation of out-groups, both a simple and yet complex group formation. It's simple in that this group formation has existed over past generations and is commonly recognized. Yet, it's complex to understand and embrace. The out-group formation dynamic is created during childhood and young adult periods and can carry forward in one's life. The formation dynamic may include categorization by abilities, e.g. intellectual vs athletic, perceived looks, odd interest associations, or non-conforming friends. Indeed, we refer to the creation of popular cliques and those who are outside of the norm as not accepted. This same group formation behavior is also seen and present in organizations.

The out-group categorization seen in organizations is triggered by those who cannot identify with the values, beliefs, or norms of those with whom they work. For example, into this categorization would fall the individual who works on a production line and wants to place a religious picture or figure in their workplace. While at first glance it may seem this practice should not be seen as an out-group trigger, it may become so if the workers around these individuals begin to make fun of the practice and separate themselves from this individual. The act of making fun of the practice can create a bond between those who do the criticizing—in-group—as well as creating an out-group who display the behavior. The results of this out-group creation can, and usually does, lead to negative personal performance and overall reduction in production output.

A much more subtle reason for out-group formation within organizations can come from the feeling of unknown exclusion. For example, new employees or even long-tenured employees who are considered "non-contributors or burdens" by the rest of the employees might experience this feeling. In either case, an out-group can be formed that knows they are excluded but do not know why. An example of an organizational treatment that becomes a trigger for creating an out-group may be as simple as who gets invited to lunch. The member of the out-group has no idea why they are excluded, other than they are. In this case, the unknown causal factor is most insidious and can be one of the most difficult to overcome (Northouse, 2018).

When leaders are attempting to pivot the organization to one that embraces diversity and adopts an inclusive culture, they must understand that out-group strategies must be a part of their overall effort to ensure the goal is met. They additionally must remember that this move takes a personal commitment by the leader to adopt personal values and behaviors that will demonstrate the organization's commitment.

5.6 INCLUSIVENESS

To understand what it means to be an included member of a diverse workgroup, let's examine the **inclusion** experience of an individual. The inclusion experience goes beyond the workplace to the whole of an individual's experiential domain. Whether an employee feels included in a workgroup will depend on the richness of experiences outside the workplace. To visualize this concept see figure 5.1, which illustrates that the inclusive experience starts with the individual and evolves as the individual experiences inclusive events in larger and more impersonal settings. After gathering inclusive experiences at the initial levels, the individual begins to interact with organizations. As a member of an organization, an individual brings with them their past experiences with inclusion and exclusion, which creates expectations around future inter-relations within the workplace (Fredman and Deane, 2013).

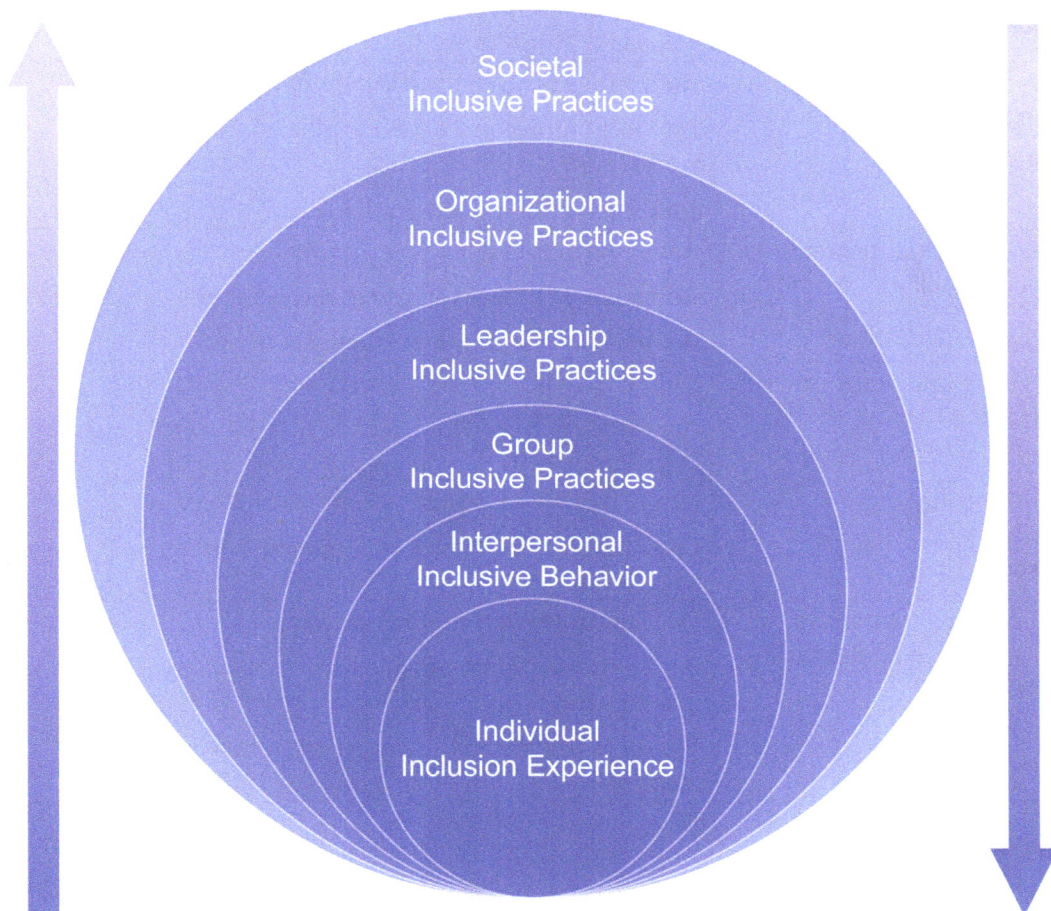

Figure 5.1: The Individual Inclusive Experience
Source: The Practice of Inclusion in Diverse Organizations, p 17
Attribution: Corey Parson, adapted from B. M. Ferdman
License: Fair Use

The individual, as a member of an organization, uses their experiences to evaluate the leadership's behavior concerning diversity and the organization's culture, values, and philosophy as they relate to diversity. The individual will evaluate the leader's behavior based upon communications, invitations to be a part of things, organizational policy, procedures, training opportunities, and ultimately promotional opportunities. The organization's new employees may use this experiential understanding of inclusion to determine whether the organization's culture, leadership, and workgroups embrace inclusive practices that warrant continued association. The inclusion experience (table 5.1) is a lifelong process that continues to evolve and mature (Fredman and Deane, 2013).

Table 5.1: Components of the Inclusion Experience

Feeling safe (self and group)	Do I feel physically and psychologically safe?
	Do I feel secure that I am a full member of the group?
	Do I feel that my contribution will be respected and valued?
Feeling involved and engaged	Am I a fully accepted participant in workgroup actions?
	Do I feel I have equal access to all resources of the workgroup?
	Do I feel part of a collaborative team?
Feeling respected and valued (self and group)	Am I being treated the way I would like to be treated?
	Do members of the workgroup respect me?
	Do others of the workgroup care about me?
Feeling influential on decision making	Do I listen when considering important decisions?
	Are my ideas considered, and do they influence decisions in my group?
Feeling authentic – bringing one's whole self to work	Can I honestly be myself with my workgroup?
	Can I have an open and honest dialogue with my workgroup?
Validating that diversity is recognized, attended to, and honored	Does my organization value diversity?
	Can my organization openly discuss and share ideas on diversity issues?
	Are there barriers in the organization based on my identity?

Source: The Practice of Inclusion in Diverse Organizations, p 38.
Attribution: B. M. Ferdman
License: Fair Use

5.7 THE INCLUSIVE ORGANIZATION

Thomas and Ely (1996) identify three organizational paradigm shifts in understanding and acceptance that need to take place for the organization to learn and adopt an inclusive **group-identity** culture:

- The discrimination-fairness legal paradigm, which is focused on assimilation and conformity between race and gender, as well as other softer categories.

- The access-and-legitimacy paradigm is "predicated on the acceptance and a celebration of differences" (Thomas and Ely, 1996, p. 5). External factors, like a change in client diversity, push the organization to react by changing its level of workforce diversity to match its new and diverse client base.

- The learning-and-effectiveness paradigm is the integration of workforce to clients, a merger, based on like perspectives and cultural backgrounds. It comprises a culture mix of the workforce and clients that will indicate the product and service needs of a company's diverse client base to its leadership.

More concretely, an organization may become more diverse and inclusive in the following ways:

1. Leadership should adopt the discrimination-fairness legal paradigm and work with their organization's members to embrace an inclusive environment for all employees.

2. Working with management at all levels, leadership should ensure that hiring processes and new employees understand and apply the fairness doctrine and embrace cultural diversity as an organizational norm and value.

3. Leaders should make sure that the new hiring processes align the organization's workforce with its clients' diverse cultures.

4. The last paradigm, learning-and-effectiveness, requires that all of the organization's members understand the new strategy and that an inclusive environment is necessary. The cultural shift to this last paradigm includes embracing the diversity of the client base.

Throughout this conversion to be a fully inclusive organizational culture, leadership should continually evaluate and monitor progress and should encourage employees through examples and messaging. They should make clear to all members of the organization the strategic importance of this new culture to the viability of the organization. This task requires proactive leadership that is devoted to creating an inclusive environment.

5.8 INCLUSIVE LEADERSHIP

To achieve an inclusive culture raises the question of what leadership theory is and what attributes are necessary to attain this goal. To answer this question we will first look at Heifetz and Laurie's (1999) research, which offers a leadership framework that is founded on the concept of **adaptive work**. Adaptive work is, in essence, the ability for the leader to recognize difficult organizational problems, like the conversion to an inclusive culture, as a "situation" and not a technical issue. Solving technical issues is only driven by a rational decision-making process directed by leadership. These kinds of "situations," on the other hand, are of such magnitude that, if leadership were to use the day-to-day decision-making norms and procedures, the result could, at a minimum, be destructive or, worse, catastrophic. Heifetz and Laurie (1999) explain:

> Adaptive work is tough on everyone. For leaders, it's counterintuitive. Rather than providing solutions, you must ask tough questions and leverage employees' collective intelligence. Instead of maintaining norms, you must challenge the "way we do business." And rather than quelling conflict, you need to draw issues out and let people feel the sting of reality (p. 36).

As Heifez and Laurie (1999) point out, the leader's role is to facilitate the situation's solution but not necessarily to direct it. If we look at the adaptive leader's action in table 5.2, we can see that adaptive leadership does not center on the leader as key decision-maker, but rather as the situation facilitator. Heifetz and Laurie (1999) also provide six adaptive leadership principles (table 5.3) as a guide that leaders can use to approach this "situation" of creating an organizational culture. These principles stress the fact that leadership confronting large scale adaptive challenges, like creating an inclusive organization, needs to utilize all of the people in the organization.

Table 5.2: Adaptive Work Calls for Leadership

Leader's Responsibilities	Type of Situation	
	Technical or Routine	*Adaptive*
Direction	Define problems and provide solutions	Identify the adaptive challenge and frame key questions and issues
Protection	Shield the organization from external threats	Let the organization feel external pressures within a range it can stand
Orientation	Clarify roles and responsibilities	Challenge current roles and resist pressure to define new roles quickly
Managing Conflict	Restore order	Expose conflict or let it emerge
Shaping Norms	Maintain norms	Challenge unproductive norms
In the course of regulating people's distress, a leader faces several key responsibilities and may have to use his or her authority differently depending on the type of work situation.		

Source: *Harvard Business Review*, "The Work of Leadership"
Attribution: Ronald Laurie and Donald L. Heifetz
License: Fair Use

Table 5.3: Adaptive Situation Principles for Leaders	
Get on the balcony	Move back and forth between being a participant in situation resolution actions and being an observer
Identify your adaptive challenge	Work with others to identify an adaptive challenge
Regulate distress	Control the parameters of the challenge for the people who are involved in the solution, e.g. control the intensity of debate and tension, clarify assumptions, help define key issues and values, control the rate and amount of change
Maintain disciplined attention	Encourage focus, not distractions or blaming; look for root causes only, and demonstrate collaboration in problem-solving
Give the work back to the employees	Instill collective self-confidence, support out of the box and independent thinking, and risk- taking without fear of failure or reprisal. Acknowledge that the employees and their ideas contain the solution
Protect leadership voices from below	"Don't silence whistle-blowers, creative deviants, and others exposing contradictions within your company. Their perspectives can provoke fresh thinking."

Source: *Harvard Business Review*, "The Work of Leadership"
Attribution: Ronald Laurie and Donald L. Heifetz
License: Fair Use

5.9 INCLUSIVE LEADERSHIP PRACTICES AND TRAITS

So far in this chapter, we have covered the definitions of diversity and inclusion as they apply to organizations. We have also delved further into the concept of organizational inclusion, describing theoretically how an inclusive leader and organization can evolve to reach their full potential. Indeed, achieving this leadership goal is a challenge requiring a motivated, trusted, and adaptable leader. Let us now examine what that leader should look like by exploring several leadership practices and traits being used to enhance inclusivity in organizations.

5.9.1 Leadership Practices

Groysberg and Connolly (2014) surveyed leaders in 24 major corporations across the world, analyzing employee statistics, third-party recognition, knowledge of corporate leadership diversity and inclusiveness views, and progression towards reaching diversity and inclusion (2014). In the most successfully diverse and inclusive organizations, the researchers found that those CEOs espoused creating a diverse and inclusive organizational culture as a personal mission. Their doing so correlates with our discussion above about leaders articulating a personal belief in diversity and inclusion. Findings revealed that these CEOs prioritized diversity and inclusion for two reasons: as a business imperative to stay competitive and as a personal moral objective based upon personal values and experience.

More generally, and aside from strong leadership buy-in, Groysberg and Connolly (2014) found the following eight leadership practices to make the most difference in creating diverse and inclusive organizations:

1. **Measure diversity and inclusion.**

   As management theorist Peter Drucker pointed out, "if you can't measure it, you can't improve it" added to the flipside thought that "you can't manage what you can't measure." The 24 CEOs from the Groysberg and Connolly (2014) research agreed. To be successful, a leader must be dedicated to measuring progress towards diversity and inclusion goals, milestones, and objectives.

2. **Hold managers accountable.**

   Diversity goals are not only organizational goals but also personal performance goals. It is up to the leader to lead by example and hold both his staff accountable and themselves accountable as well. Everyone in the organization must understand that diversity and inclusion are part of their job and are their responsibilities.

3. **Support flexible work arrangements.**

   Diverse people have diverse lives; with that inherent trait comes the need for flexibility in work environments. To be fully inclusive, leaders must understand and acknowledge their employees' diverse needs and put into place policies that are flexible enough to meet everyone's requirements.

4. **Recruit and promote from diverse pools of candidates.**

   Hiring and promoting practices, such as applicant mixes, hiring patterns, and promotional activities and retention rates by diversity category, are measurable metrics that should become part of leadership and performance reviews. Retention in diversity groups, for example, may be a good indicator of the degree of inclusivity in an organization's culture.

5. **Provide leadership education.**

   Leadership education on diversity and inclusion is not a one-time event but a continuous educational process. The organizational culture should evolve as leadership theory and practice evolve. This education should be available for everyone, from the senior staff members to the less experienced employees.

6. **Sponsor employee resource groups and mentoring programs.**

Leadership needs to sponsor and support the creation of employee groups that center on work tasks and resource sharing, such as with employee networking groups. Moreover, mentoring programs offer two features that support a diversity effort. Mentees get an opportunity to observe and participate in organizational actions that they may not otherwise access. These programs also enhance overall communication and messaging within the organization through the mentor/mentee relationships.

7. **Offer quality role models.**

It is important that new and diverse employees see role models that reflect the variety found within the organization. For example, Jim Rogers, the CEO of Duke Energy, explained, "This historically has been a man's industry. So, early on, we worked to move a woman into a plant manager position. That set an example. You have to be intentional and make sure you populate your organization with leaders who represent diversity. That creates an environment that allows those with diverse backgrounds to say, 'If they can, I can.' That is a very important feeling that needs to be embedded in the people in the company" (Groysberg and Connolly, 2014).

8. **Make the chief diversity officer position count.**

Groysberg and Connolly (2014) found that the CEOs they surveyed made the Chief Diversity Officers part of the executive board and had them provide direct reports to the CEO. The relationship between the Chief Diversity Officer and the CEO must be open and honest at all times. This relationship will set an example of diversity within the organization.

While the organizational leaders who employ these eight best practices and personally espouse diversity and inclusiveness values will have a "leg up" on other leaders, there are certain talents and personal qualities that the most successful leaders will have and/or develop to help create diversity in organizations.

5.10 INCLUSIVE LEADERSHIP TRAITS

Dillon and Bourke (2016) analyzed leadership traits of successfully inclusive leaders in the always-evolving context and environment that we live in currently. As a starting point, Dillon and Bourke (2016) provided key conceptual elements on what it means to be inclusive (see table 5.4). These elements reflect components of inclusiveness discussed earlier in this chapter: fairness and respect between all members of an organization; value and belonging, which applies to all within an organization; and confidence and inspiration, which removes the fear of risk-taking and increases motivation.

Table 5.4: Elements of Inclusion

Fairness and Respect	Value and belonging	Confidence and inspiration
Foundational elements that is underpinned by ideas about equality of treatment and opportunities	Individuals feeling that their uniqueness is known and appreciated while also feeling a sense of social connectedness and group membership.	Creating the conditions for high team performance through individuals having the confidence to speak up and the motivation to do their best work.

Source: The six signature traits of inclusive leadership
Attribution: Dillion and Bourke
License: Fair Use

They then identified six signature traits of inclusive leadership (table 5.5).

Table 5.5: Six Signature Traits of an Inclusive Leader

Six Traits	1	2	3	4	5	6
	Commitment	Courage	Cognizance of bias	Curiosity	Cultural Intellegence	Collaboration
	Personal values	Humility	Self-Regulation	Openess	Drive	Empowerment
15 Elements	Belief in business case	Bravery	Fair play	Perspective-taking	Knowledge	Teaming
				Coping with ambiguity	Adaptability	Voice

Source: The six signature traits of inclusive leadership
Attribution: Dillion and Bourke
License: Fair Use

5.10.1 Commitment

Commitment, per Dillion and Bourke, means that "highly inclusive leaders are committed to diversity and inclusion because these objectives align with their personal values and because they believe in the business case" (2016). Leaders should internalize a commitment to inclusive values into their personal values. Indeed, if that personal value is strong enough, then there will be equally strong confidence to interweave diversity and inclusive practices into the overall organizational vision and execution.

5.10.2 Courage

According to Dillion and Bourke, "highly inclusive leaders speak up and challenge the status quo, and they are humble about their strengths and weaknesses" (2016).

Courage means holding on to personal values in the face of strong opposition and complicated situations, and involves challenging conventional wisdom and acknowledging our own shortfalls. The inclusive leader needs this level of courage and humility to address personal and organizational biases and prejudices.

5.10.3 Cognizance of Bias

The next trait, cognizance of bias, means that "highly inclusive leaders are mindful of personal and organizational blind spots, and self-regulate to help ensure 'fair play'" (Dillon and Bourke, 2016, p. 11). In addressing cultural bias, the leader needs to humbly yet boldly be the advocate of the diverse population, thus empowering and encouraging diverse populations within workgroups to contribute and openly engage in the organization's business. As part of the effort to eliminate organizational bias, the leader needs to offer proactive support of equal treatment to all members of the organization (Dillon and Bourke, 2016).

5.10.4 Curiosity

Dillon and Bourke also state that "Highly inclusive leaders have an open mindset, a desire to understand how others view and experience the world, and a tolerance for ambiguity" (2016). As an example, attempting to achieve the Thomas and Ely (1996) access-and-legitimacy paradigm, previously discussed in this chapter, requires leadership curiosity. In this last evolutionary inclusive paradigm, the culturally diverse client base would "dovetail" with the organization's diverse workforce to create a new communication channel, a channel where clients in conjunction with the workforce would define culturally diverse products and services. To accomplish this goal, leadership will be equally interested in wanting to become knowledgeable of such diverse clients, as they used to be with the more traditional clients of the past. It will be the level of leadership's curiosity traits that drive the success of this step (Dillion and Bourke, 1996).

5.10.5 Culturally Intelligent

As leaders successfully evolve in external and internal environments, they demonstrate that "Highly inclusive leaders are confident and effective in cross-cultural interactions." Besides acquiring knowledge, leaders need to use this knowledge and personally engage in the cultural exchange that is taking place within their organizations. Given the rapidly changing product and service demand of diverse clients, leaders who cannot or will not attempt to understand these new cross-cultural interactions will fail (Dillion and Bourke, 1996).

5.10.6 Collaborative

Dillion and Bourke (1996) note that "Highly inclusive leaders empower individuals as well as create and leverage the thinking of diverse groups" (1996).

Leaders need to use their personal values of inclusion to encourage, empower, and engage diverse members of their organizations to trust, contribute, take risks, communicate, and contribute to their organizations. Doing this requires that both leaders and diverse members develop an openness at all levels.

5.11 LEADERSHIP AND ORGANIZATION BARRIERS TO ACHIEVING DIVERSITY AND INCLUSIVENESS

The concluding section of this chapter will of necessity address—at least briefly—the barriers in both leadership and organizations in achieving an inclusive organizational culture.

5.11.1 Unique Barrier: The Out-Groups

As discussed above, it is the out-group's presence that creates a special leadership challenge, particularly when the organization is needing to embrace and create an inclusive culture as outlined above. Northouse (2018) presents a basic leadership strategy to address the issue of out-groups, noting that a leader must first recognize and develop a personal value statement and understanding to address this dilemma. He points out this five-step strategic approach:

1. Listen to out-group members

2. Show empathy to out-group members

3. Recognize the unique contributions of out-group members

4. Create a special relationship with out-group members

5. Give out-group members a voice and empower them to act

In all cases, leaders must assure out-group members that they, as the leaders, will protect the communication channel not only privately but also publicly.

5.11.2 Personal Values and Practical Barriers

Many of these examples of barriers represent common experiences, and most people will be very aware of their existence. Indeed, this chapter has been devoted to correcting or mitigating these barriers. Some barriers can be classified as personal issues; others are grounded in the practical aspects of the organization (table 5.6).

Table 5.6: Barriers to Diversity and Inclusion

Personal Value Barriers	Practical Barriers
Resistance to Change – fear of change, threat to employment, status quo bias	Communication Barriers – organizational structure issues that are based on non-diverse considerations, e.g. childcare
In-Group Favoritism – creation of "out-group" either socially or organizationally	Wage Equity – fear of abruptly changing employment status and compensation biases
Cognitive Biases and Stereotyping – a narrow view of who is different and an unwillingness to learn about others	Interpersonal Miscommunication and Conflict - cultural barriers in the form of accents, wording, or an unwillingness to understand someone who is considered different
Homophily - the tendency of individuals to associate with others who are similar to them	Difficulty in Defining Diversity – unclear organizational definition of what and how diversity is and how it will be applied. Does the company's definition of diversity address all categories of physical differences as well as work skills and personality types as groups who will be viewed equally by leadership?

Source: Boundless Management. "Challenges to Achieving Diversity"
Attribution: Lumen
License: Fair Use

These barriers could have been addressed early in this chapter; however, it is hoped that first discussing diversity, inclusive leadership strategies, and behaviors has led to a better understanding of these barriers as well as how to address them.

5.12 APPLICATION PROFILE

Brian Krzanich, CEO of Intel – Leading by Example

During his tenure at CEO of Intel, Brian Krzanich made headlines several times for his move to diversify the company staff of over 100,000 worldwide employees.

Early during his tenure at Intel, Krzanich announced a $300 million five-year plan to bring the company's workforce to "full representation" by 2020. "It's time to step up and do more," Krzanich said. "It's not just good enough to say we value diversity, and then have our workplaces and our industry not reflect the full availability and talent pool of women and underrepresented minorities."

From there, Krzanich put into place a multipronged effort to increase diverse hires, including a $4,000 employee referral bonus and a $5 million partnership to develop a high school computer science curriculum for local school districts.

In June, the company published a 15-page statistical report on whether or not these investments were working. The result: The actual number of diverse hires by

June was up to 1,275 employees in the U.S. With the original goal set at 40% for the year, Intel surpassed that in six months, with 43.3% of their new hires falling into the diverse category.

5.13 SUMMARY

This chapter addressed the question of organizational diversity and inclusion from a leadership position. As previously defined, leadership is "the action of leading a group of people or an organization" (Oxford University). Leadership in this context is an all-inclusive identification of anyone in an organization who has responsibility for not only defining tasks but also for looking after the welfare and direction of other people who are also helping to accomplish these tasks. With this approach, the content of this chapter defines and reviews the concept of diversity and inclusion as a changing norm of historical culture within an organization and society in general. As a further extension of this effort, we discussed a brief review of leadership theory as it has attempted to embrace this new cultural norm as an organizational leadership element.

Heifetz and Laurie's (1999) research in the *Work of Leadership* posits an adaptive leadership framework. We discussed this framework as a means to understand how this cultural norming requires leaders to practice adaptive methods to direct organizations in embracing the need to be diverse, as well as influencing group behavior within the organization to include those who are considered different. This process included a discussion of "out-groups," considering who they are, how they are identified, and what are their models and methods of inclusion. As we previously pointed out, this area is one of the most difficult leadership challenges at all levels of the organizational hierarchy. We then used the adaptive method to focus on leadership responsibilities in all phases of diversity/inclusive communication and decision-making practices.

The final part of the chapter looked at examples of where diversity and inclusion leadership works and provided some pointers on how to introduce the concept in a company setting. Groysberg and Connolly's (2014) research identified eight leadership practices that make a difference in the organization:

1. Measure diversity and inclusion.

2. Hold managers accountable.

3. Support flexible work arrangements.

4. Recruit and promote from diverse pools of candidates.

5. Provide leadership education.

6. Sponsor employee resource groups and mentoring programs.

7. Offer quality role models.

8. Make the chief diversity officer position count.

As the chapter points out, all of these practices are important; however, it takes the organization's head to lead by example in their execution, thus sustaining these practices as they are culturally embraced by the organization.

The following chapter will bridge our discussion from leadership theory, through foundational principles, and into practices. It will consider the practices that address both long term and current leadership issues relating to the question of how leadership creates a mantel of trust not only through behavior but also in the ability to recognize the value of all the organization's members to address conflict. This question is a significant challenge for anyone who aspires to be a good leader.

5.14 DISCUSSION QUESTIONS

1. Discuss organizational diversity and inclusion.
2. Evaluate the evolution of diversity and inclusion as applied to leadership and organizations.
3. Discuss inclusive leadership strategies.
4. What practical leadership methods can be used to create a diverse and inclusive environment?
5. What is the nature of an out-group? Does this set fall under a different categorization? What leadership strategies can be used to address this organizational issue?

5.15 FURTHER READING

Cottrill, Kenna, Patricia Denise Lopez, and Calvin C. Hoffman. "How authentic leadership and inclusion benefit organizations." *Equality, Diversity and Inclusion: An International Journal* 33, no. 3,2014.

Ferdman, Bernardo M. and Deane, Barbara R. (ed.). *Diversity at Work: The Practice of Inclusion.* Germany: Wiley, 2013.

Leyens, Jacques-Philippe, Paola M. Paladino, Ramon Rodriguez-Torres, Jeroen Vaes, Stéphanie Demoulin, Armando Rodriguez-Perez, and Ruth Gaunt. "The Emotional Side of Prejudice: The Attribution of Secondary Emotions to Ingroups and Outgroups." *Personality and Social Psychology Review* 4, no. 2. May 2000, 186–97. doi:10.1207/S15327957PSPR0402_06.

Maslow, Abraham H. *Toward a Psychology of Being.* United States: Start Publishing LLC, 2013.

Riggio, Ronald (2014, January 22) What Is Authentic Leadership? Do You Have It? *Psychology Today, January 22, 2014.* https://www.psychologytoday.com/us/blog/cutting-edge-leadership/201401/what-is-authentic-leadership-do-you-have-it.

5.16 REFERENCES

Boundless Management. "Challenges to Achieving Diversity".. Lumen. N/A Accessed November 15, 2019. https://courses.lumenlearning.com/boundless-management/chapter/challenges-to-achieving-diversity/.

Dillion, Bernadette and Bourke, Juliet). "The six signature traits of inclusive leadership: Thriving in a diverse new world." April16, 2016. Accessed December 5, 2019. https://www2.deloitte.com/content/dam/insights/us/articles/six-signature-traits-of-inclusive-leadership/DUP-3046_Inclusive-leader_vFINAL.pdf.

Dishman, Lydia. "Millennials have a different definition of diversity and inclusion." May 18, 2015. Access from http:// www.fastcompany.com/ 3046358/ the-new-rules-of-work/ millennials-have-a-different-definition-of-diversity-and-inclusion.

Dishman, Lydia. "A Brief History of Diversity Training." June 18, 2018. Access December 16, 2019

https://www.fastcompany.com/40579246/a-brief-history-of-diversity-training.

Ferdman, B. M. "The practice of inclusion in diverse organizations: Toward a systemic and inclusive framework." In *The professional practice series. Diversity at work: The practice of inclusion*, edited by B. M. Ferdman & B. R. Deane, 3–54. Jossey-Bass, 2014. https://doi.org/10.1002/9781118764282.ch1.

Groysberg, Boris, and Katherine Connolly. "Great Leaders Who Make the Mix Work." *Harvard Business Review*, October 27, 2014. https://hbr.org/2013/09/great-leaders-who-make-the-mix-work.

Laurie, Ronald and Heifetz, Donald L. "The Work of Leadership." *Harvard Business Review*, March 18, 2019. http://www.kwli.org/wp-content/uploads/2015/01/Heifetz-Laurie-2001.pdf.

Northouse, Peter G. *Introduction to Leadership: Concepts and Practices, 4th ed.* Los Angles: SAGE Publications, 2018.

Oxford English Dictionary online Google Edition, https://www.google.com/h?q=definition+of+leadership&oq=definition+of+leadership&aqs=chrome..69i57j0l6j69i60.9537j1j4&sourceid=chrome&ie=UTF-8.

Thomas, D. A., & Ely, R. J. "Making differences matter: A new paradigm for managing diversity". *Harvard Business Review*, September– October, 1996. Access from https://store.hbr.org/product/making-differences-matter-a-new-paradigm-for-managing-diversity/96510?sku=96510-HCB-ENG.

6

Challenges to Organizational and Ethical Leadership, Conflict Resolution

6.1 LEARNING OBJECTIVES

After this chapter students will

1. Describe moral ethics and how they are related to organizational leadership, character, and behavior

2. Explain what a conflict environment is and its relationship with ethical leadership decisions and behavior

3. Understand ethical leadership practices and conflict management

4. Describe and understand Fisher and Ury's ideas about effective negotiation as a means of resolving conflict

5. Understand the Kilmann and Thomas "Styles of Approaching Conflict" in leadership decision-making and conflict resolution

6. Understand how examples of ethical leadership in managing conflict can impact overall organizational culture

6.2 KEY TERMS

- Morality
- Conscientious
- Inclusive
- Accountable
- Considerate
- Consistent
- Authoritative
- Relational conflict
- Content conflict

- Principled negotiation
- Thomas Kilmann Conflict Model (TKI)

6.3 INTRODUCTION

Not all conflicts are destructive and dysfunctional to an organization. Likewise, not all leaders can be classified in only two categories, ethical or unethical; they may be at times both or neither. This chapter will first take up the subject of ethics in a general overview and then apply the following understanding to leaders and leadership behavior. The second part of this chapter will address a situation in which ethical leadership behaviors can be put to the test in organizational conflicts. With this section, we will look at a general definition of conflict and how it is used to describe organizational situations. The last section will also analyze leadership ethical practices against an organization's conflictual dynamics.

John Maxwell, Ethics 101 (2003)

> *One of our problems is that ethics is never a business issue or a social issue or a political issue. It is always a personal issue.*

6.4 ETHICS

6.4.1 Principles of Leadership Ethics

If we take Maxwell's (2003) statement that there is no such thing as topical ethics but only the notion of ethics and its characterization of **morality** seriously, then it is easy to say that there is no true concept of leadership ethics. Indeed, to continue Maxwell's thought, ethics is always a "personal issue" based on personal values and beliefs. He states that "some companies have given up entirely on trying to figure out what's ethical and are instead using what's legal as the standard for decision-making. The result is moral bankruptcy" (9). In chapter 5, we saw that to be considered an inclusive leader one must be committed to creating a diverse and inclusive organizational culture, which begins with the leader's personal values and beliefs, along with their ethical value propositions. Applying Maxwell's critique to this idea, then, reveals that an ethical leader is also one who does not succumb to the convenience of using a legal structure to replace an ethical organization.

6.4.2 Characteristics of Ethical Leadership

Ethical leaders have several characteristics, or traits, in common, according to many studies (Brown and Trevino, 2006; Northhouse, 2018; Kalshoven, Den Hartog, & De Hoogh, 2011). These attributes describe the leaders themselves and how they are perceived by the organization, as evidenced by what the leaders say and do. See table 6.1.

Table 6.1: Attributes/Traits of an Ethical Leader

Attribute	Descriptor
Conscientious	• Diligent and aware of their actions, especially towards others
	• Does not waver in the pursuit of making and taking the right actions
	• Personal values are displayed in the leader's messages and actions
Inclusive	• The ethical leader must genuinely care about their organization's members and best interests, as well as the organization itself
	• A leader will demonstrate enabling methods that include all members of the organization in decision making considerations
Accountable	• A leader's character is demonstrated as being transparent through their being held accountable
	• Build trust in the organization, admitting errors, and demonstrating attempts to correct past actions
	• Act as the ethical role model for all members of the organization
Considerate	• Address and treat all members of the organization on equal terms
	• Show equal treatment to alternative decisions and solutions
Consistent	• Ability to create and hold accountable standards that are equally fair to all members of the organization
	• Ethical treatment is equal to all members of the organization regardless of their professional station
Authoritative	• Be the key decision-maker in the organization and be inclusive with input from the organization's members in regard to future and ongoing decisions or actions
	• Demonstrate through messaging and action that ethical behavior is the primary organizational value
	• "Walk the talk"

Source: Ethical Leadership Guide
Attribution: Ethical Leadership Guide
License: Fair Use

Conscientious

Conscientiousness is the commitment to hold to a standard, especially a personal standard. A conscientious ethical leader is concerned about all their actions. This definition of conscientious behavior is framed in Peter Drucker's commonly quoted phrase describing the difference between management and leadership: "management is doing things right, leadership is doing the right thing," regardless of the consequences. This diligence in action can attest to an ethical leader's character.

An example of a conscientious leader is Mike Valentine, President & CEO of Illinois based Baxter Credit Union (BCU). BCU also has several locations in Puerto

Rico. On September 17, 2017, when Hurricane Maria struck, both CEO Valentine and BCU demonstrated Drucker's example of conscientious leadership. As we now know, the devastation to Puerto Rico by this hurricane was monumental. Most, if not many, private companies, especially financial institutions, were shuttered or non-existent after the storm. Through CEO Valentine's leadership and the BCU Puerto Rican employees' "resolve," the company took the opposite action and remained open, thereby putting "the needs of members above their own."

BCU took aggressive action by keeping their ATMs stocked with money so all victims, not just BCU members, could withdraw cash without fees. It was also one of the first to issue 0% interest disaster-recovery loans, defer interest payments on existing loans, and accept hand-written promissory notes of repayment for cash distribution while the network was non-functional. All of these decisions were contrary to not only company policy and procedure but also to industry standards. Indeed, CEO Valentine stated, "My only thought was to do everything humanly possible to ensure the safety of our employees and meet member needs" (Weinstein, 2019). This unconventional but conscientiously ethical action by CEO Valentine not only meets Drucker's standard that "leadership is doing the right thing;" it also had the effect of increasing membership by 20% and leading to expanded operations for the company.

Inclusive

As we discussed in chapter 5, inclusion is one key goal of an effective organization. The characteristics that make an ethically inclusive leader include the following:

- Openness to others' thoughts, ideas, and opinions, while also encouraging all members of the organization to express their thoughts
- Commitment, through words and actions, to inclusiveness
- Collaborative environment for all diverse members, recognizing uniqueness
- Creation of educational goals for all members of the organization; education is a continuous activity
- Listening to individuals, groups, and the entire organization without judgment or bias
- Courage in demonstrating a willingness to break down existing cultural barriers within the organization, as well as recognizing their own limitations and showing humility through seeking the advice of others (Dillion and Bourke 2016; Ethical Leadership Guide, 2016).

Accountable

When applied to ethical leadership, **accountability** is not just a personal accounting of responsibility; it also includes responsibility for the whole organization. An ethical leader who demonstrates transparent accountability is a leader who acknowledges that issues and failings of the organization are their responsibility, as are the consequences of their own actions. They become the ethical role model for the organization and its workforce.

The adage that "the captain goes down with the ship" captures the essence of ethical leadership accountability. In the news, we often have unfortunately witnessed just the opposite of this ethical leadership accountability. Think of Enron's chairman, Ken Lay, denying wrongdoing and asserting he was unaware of the fraudulent accounting practices occurring on his watch. Demonstrating accountability builds trust within the organization and between the organization and its constituents.

Considerate

Being **considerate** entails showing equal concern for others or treating everyone with equal respect. It does not, however, mean that everyone is equal in their roles and responsibilities in the organization. Rather, considerate leader values all members of the organization equally. In the eyes of the ethical leader, each member is a valuable contributor in their role. For instance, an ethical leader would not assign a major research and development project to an employee who was brought into the organization to work as a call center agent. The ethical leader may show consideration, however, by equally soliciting ideas and thoughts from all members of the entire organization who may have client knowledge, such as would a call center agent. In this case, the research and development project leader and the call center agent are equally valued in the development of new products or services.

The second dimension to consider is doing no harm. Simple as it sounds, it may be one of the most challenging aspects of being an ethically considerate leader. The complexity here arises when the chosen decision will harm regardless of the action taken. Messick and Bazerman (1996) suggest three criteria (table 6.2) that can improve the decision-making process for leaders when they are trying their best to do no harm (Ethical Leadership Guide, 2016).

Table 6.2: Criteria for Considerate, Ethical Decision-Making

Criteria	Actions
Quality	Ensuring that all of an action's consequences are considered. It implies having accurate assessments of the risks associated with possible strategies and being attuned to the pitfalls of egocentric biases.
Breadth	Assessing the full range of consequences that policies may entail. An ethical audit of a decision must consider the outcomes for all stakeholders (including all members of the organization as well as clients and vendors). The first task is to compile a list of stakeholders. The second is to evaluate a decision's likely outcomes from the stakeholders' perspective. It means doing the right thing and doing the smart thing.
Honesty	Practicing a policy of openness driven by conscience and disclosure. Consider the "sunshine test": how would one feel if they saw their decision on the front page of the New York Times? Consider if the stakeholders would accept the decision; consider the question "whether the people with the most to lose would accept the reasons for our actions."

Source: "Ethical leadership and the psychology of decision making", *MIT Sloan Management Review*
Attribution: Messick and Bazerman
License: Fair Use

Consistent

An ethical leader must be **consistent** and steady in their personal values and the application of these values. If this consistency of purpose wavers, the leader risks losing a bond of trust between themself and the organization. This personal conviction is even more important in the face of adversarial situations. The ethical leader must manifest the same level of consistency in their relationships with all members of the organization as they do with holding true to their values.

Authoritative

Authoritative ethical leadership recognizes power. How that power is demonstrated, though, is what sets the ethical leader apart from others. Let us clarify the various aspects of power. Table 6.3 presents six bases of power as posited by French and Raven (1959). These areas can be used to assess and create a composite of ethical leadership authority.

Table 6.3: French and Raven's Five Forms of Power

Forms	Description	Example
Legitimate	This comes from the belief that a person has the formal right to make demands and to expect others to be compliant and obedient.	A teacher who evaluates student performance toward the course requirements.
Reward	This results from one person's ability to compensate another for compliance.	Employer/supervisor/manager who can provide wages and benefits.
Expert	This is based on a person's high levels of skill and knowledge.	A person who may have strong knowledge of organizational processes, software, or product development.
Referent	This is the result of a person's perceived attractiveness, worthiness, and right to others' respect.	A person who is liked for various personal qualities, e.g. popular or helpful.
Coercive	This comes from the belief that a person can punish others for noncompliance.	A school principal who can hold students accountable and punish them for noncompliant behavior.
Informational (added six years later)	This results from a person's ability to control the information that others need to accomplish something.	A person in an organization who possesses or can grant access to information that others are dependent on, a database manager.

Source: Five Forms of Power
Attribution: French and Raven
License: Fair Use

Clearly, authority stems from several sources. What is important to consider here in determining ethics, though, is how the leader uses these various forms. Let us consider Angela Merkel, Chancellor of Germany for 10 years. She is considered the most powerful woman in the world and has considerable authority in Germany, the European Union, and other international contexts. In 2015, Chancellor Merkel faced a massive humanitarian crisis that put her authority and power to the test. In that year, over one million Syrian refugees and migrants seeking asylum presented themselves at Germany's border seeking asylum. Amid the opposition of many citizens, other political leaders, and neighboring countries, Chancellor Merkel opened the border and began a difficult process of assimilating these individuals into Germany. She was able to make this ethical decision, despite so much resistance, because she had legitimate and referential authority and power. Her demonstrated ethical leadership was grounded in the personal values she had developed as a young girl growing up in east Germany, understanding the human need for refuge. Chancellor Merkel's leadership is an excellent example of the ethical use of a leader's authority.

These characteristics of ethical leadership have been identified in many different leaders. They embody the foundations of a personal ethical position that leaders must not only demonstrate but also find deep within themselves. To sum up the essence of ethical leadership we will use the conclusion by Subhasree (2010): "Ethical leadership is knowing your core values and having the courage to live them in all parts of your life in service of the common good" (113).

6.5 THE CONFLICT ISSUE: AN ETHICAL LEADERSHIP CHALLENGE

Conflict is the result of human interaction. Fundamentally, human conflict is a disagreement between at least two individuals over any intangible or tangible subject/object. The subject of the conflict or disagreement can range from trite to life-threatening. Conflict, per Hocker and Wilmot (2010, pp. 3-9), contains these elements:

- A struggle between two differing individuals or groups
- Involving goals, personal or group, that are incompatible
- In many cases, scarce resources are the subject of dispute
- Individuals view one another as impediments to reaching personal or group goals

Conflict is rooted in an emotional investment on the part of those involved. Conflict resolution, then, must address the emotional aspects, as well as any other tangible considerations related to the argument. Participants can be perceived as "winning" the conflict yet emotionally "feel" they have lost. Therefore, in conflict resolution, each party must understand and address both the tangible and the emotional aspects of the issue. It is a dual resolution process.

6.5.1 Communication in Conflict

The main tool in conflict resolution is communication between the parties. Communication, regardless of the medium, is the channel through which emotions move.

Studies by Watzlawick, Bevin, and Jackson (1967) point out that communication contains two dimensions, **content** and **relational**. Therefore, understanding the nature of conflict requires reviewing these communication dimensions to understand its dynamics. Using a classification illustration (figure 6.1) proposed by Northouse (2018) of the Walzlawick, et. al (1967) dimensions and their elements, a clear distinction is revealed between communication that transmits content and communication that carries the emotional components of an argument.

CONTENT CONFLICTS   RELATIONAL CONFLICTS

Regarding Beliefs and Values	Regarding Goals	Issues of Esteem	Issues of Control	Issues of Affiliation

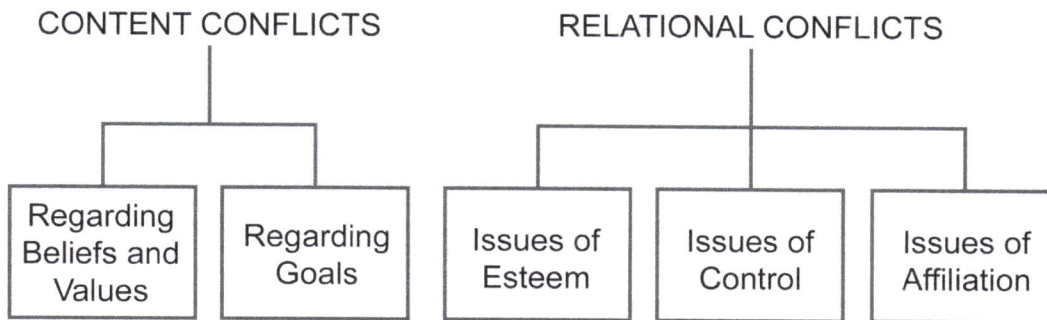

Figure 6.1: Examples of Content and Relational Conflicts
Source: Original Work
Attribution: Corey Parson, adapted from Northouse
License: Fair Use

Content messaging is the literal substance of the message, that is, the actual information that is being transmitted from one person, the sender, to the other, the receiver. The content intends to inform. But this content may also contain the sender's values, expected results, and rationale for the content. If the receiver hears the message but does not buy into the sender's values or rationale, conflict can develop. For instance, if a supervisor comments on the messiness of an employee's workspace, the message contains the supervisor's value of the organization, as well as an expected result that the employee cleans up their space. If the employee does not accept this foundational value of the supervisor and/or organization and feels like they work better in a more chaotic environment, then conflict can ensue (Walzlawick, et. al, 1967).

Communication also contains a relational dimension, which is the part of the message that can also carry emotive elements. **Relational conflicts** regard subtle aspects of communication that may be outside of the message's content but influences the message's interpretation, nonetheless. Relational conflict is based in part on how a sender and receiver feel about each other; is there a feeling of acceptance, like or dislike, comfort or discomfort? Much of relational conflict arises from non-verbal communication, such as facial expressions, body language, or the tone in a written message (Walzlawick, et. al, 1967).

Referring to the previous example of the supervisor's comment about the condition of the employee's workspace, we can see how relational content can also come into play to create conflict. The employee will hear that message but process it in the context of their relationship with the supervisor. Do they have a comfortable, open relationship? Do they joke with each other? Does the supervisor often exert their power and authority over the employee? How does the employee think that the supervisor perceives them and their work? How was the message delivered, with a smile or with a stern look? Have the employee and supervisor had a conflict in the past? All these relational factors come into play when a receiver is interpreting a message from a sender. It is important here to consider how feelings of affiliation or acceptance are critical to how the subordinate interprets their supervisor's message.

Communication, again, is the essence of conflict. Managing messaging is very important when managing conflict. Keep in mind, in a growing and evolving organization, conflict is inevitable and not necessarily negative. As Northouse (2018) argues, the way that we "manage conflict [can] produce positive change" (pp. 240-241). Therefore, the following section will address how leaders address organizational conflict and suggest some methods used in conflict management.

6.6 MANAGING CONFLICT IN PRACTICE

This section will review two methods of managing conflict in the context of ethical leadership. The first conflict management strategy is called **Principled Negotiation** and was proposed by Fisher and Ury (2011). The second method is the conflict model created by Kilmann and Thomas (1977), which considers different behavioral styles in managing conflicts.

6.6.1 Principled Negotiation

When it comes to managing conflict, especially for leadership, Fisher and Ury (2011) have proposed a method whose intent is to use a form of "win-win" negotiation that is mutually beneficial to both parties. The goal of this method is not just to resolve a conflict but to reach a resolution that reinforces and maintains a long-lasting relationship between the two conflicting parties.

Fisher and Ury (2011) propose a propositional model addressing the behavior of the parties involved in conflict negotiation. The model contains four principles (see figure 6.2), which are proposed to maximize the most positive result in conflicts between parties.

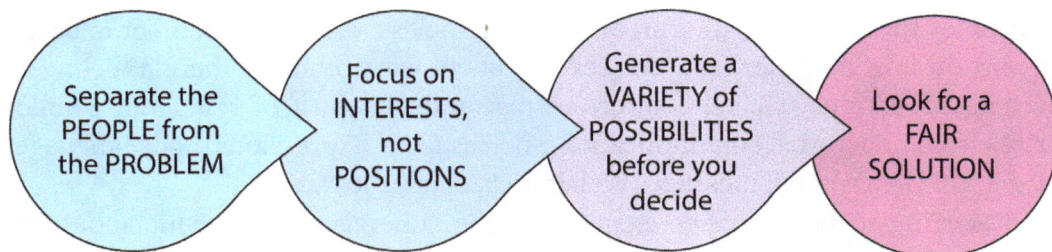

Separate the PEOPLE from the PROBLEM → Focus on INTERESTS, not POSITIONS → Generate a VARIETY of POSSIBILITIES before you decide → Look for a FAIR SOLUTION

Figure 6.2: Four Propositions of Principled Negotiation
Source: Original Work
Attribution: Corey Parson, adapted from Fisher and Ury
License: Fair Use

First Principle – Separate People from the Problem

According to Fisher and Ury, "A basic fact about negotiation, easy to forget in corporate and international transactions, is that you are dealing not with abstract representatives of the 'other side,' but with human beings" (Fisher and Ury, 2011, p. 20). As the first principle points out, we need to recognize that the conflict is between humans and the acknowledged role of the human ego. This first principle recommends removing egos from the dialogue. Effective negotiation is not a competition in which one party wins and the other loses. When egos take over the discussion, it can become personal and the conflict irreconcilable. In good negotiation, each party needs to recognize that the process contains two objectives: to resolve the point of conflict and to maintain a good relationship between the parties.

In the presentation of this principle, Fry and Ury (2011) identify these three elements for effectively applying the principle, that is, to separate the human element from the perceived problem.

Perception – It is the perception held and subsequent thinking by each party, such as ill-founded fears and unrealistic hopes, that may undermine any facts presented to solve the problem.

Emotion – Regardless of a discussion based on facts, it is the feeling held by each party that will determine the success or failure of any negotiations.

Communication – Remember that "without communication there is no negotiation" (p. 36). Barriers in negotiation communications may fall into the following two behaviors: (1) parties involved are not talking to each other but to observers, and (2) the parties are not listening to each other but only to what they will say next.

These three elements of the first principle make clear that an individual party involved in a conflict negotiation needs to focus on the personal attributes of the other party as well their own.

Second Principle – Focus on Interest and not Position

According to Fisher and Ury, "reconciling interests rather than compromising between positions also works because behind opposed positions lie many more interests than conflicting ones" (Fisher and Ury, 2011, p. 44). The second principle moves from the "people" element of the negotiation to the issue itself and the interest each party has beyond the conflict. This principle makes the negotiation less concerned with each party than with the "value" of the solution itself. This second principle focuses upon discovering a mutually workable solution through like interests. The following are suggested steps in determining the underlying interests of each party.

- Ask why the party holds the positions they do and consider why the party does not hold some other possible position.

- Explain your interests clearly.

- Discuss these interests together, looking forward to the desired solution rather than focusing on past events.

- Focus clearly on your interests but remain open to different proposals and positions (Principled Negotiation – The Harvard Approach, p. 2).

Third Principle – Invent Options for Mutual Gain

According to Fisher and Ury, "all too often negotiators 'leave money on the table,' they fail to reach an agreement when they might have, or the agreement they do reach could have been better for each side" (Fisher and Ury, 2011, p. 59). The application of this principle may be challenging since it requires mutual consideration and may be forced given the dynamics of the negotiation process. Fisher and Ury (2011) identify four obstacles in determining options for mutual benefit: (1) Being too quick to select an option, a rush to judgment, (2) Seeking a single option, (3) Negotiation must be a "win-win" scenario, and (4) Stalemated negotiation process – expectation that the resolution must be the final one.

The first barrier is being too quick to select an option, or making a rush to judgment. The suggestion is that the parties involved should be inventive but practical about the options under consideration. Will the option under consideration optimally work for both groups? A solution to this obstacle is separating option creation from the final evaluation of the options.

For example, a project team has been chartered by management from two separate functions, e.g. marketing and research/development, to recommend the most important product deliverables for the next year for the company, with two members representing each function. At a meeting held to discuss this recommendation, the members from each function propose a deliverable that favors their function as the most important. As their negotiation progresses and each side presents their case, the other side immediately critiques it and points out its shortcomings. To break this stalemate, a proposed solution is to brainstorm. All possible recommendations are solicited from each member of the team without judgment and listed. After that process is completed, all brainstormed recommendations can be discussed for clarification. After which, the entire team would use a multi-vote process to determine the best recommendation. This effort may possibly lead to a recommendation that was never considered before being selected because each member of the team can see value in the new creative recommendation for both functions.

The second obstacle is seeking a single option. As we saw in the above example, a dialogue in which every recommendation option is critiqued immediately upon its being presented leads to total inaction and no recommendation. However, by using the brainstorming method, many options can be presented and considered.

Fisher and Ury (2011) present a third obstacle, that negotiation *must* be a "win-win" scenario. As already pointed out, a solution for the "win-win" position is the agreement amongst the parties that the option chosen must contain mutual benefits to each. However, given the first two obstacles, the "win-win" solution set must discount preconceived notions of what is best for each. From the previous example, we can see that the brainstorming process led to many mutually beneficial options. Indeed, if this part of the negotiation is done correctly, the selected option may be one neither party considered when they began the original negotiation.

As the last obstacle, the authors point out that in a stalemated negotiation process, each party may expect the other to break the stalemate by coming up with the final resolution. If neither party can provide an acceptable solution, then the negotiation ends up in gridlock and the negotiation fails. However, what is needed at this point is a creative decision method. Again, turning to the example, after brainstorming, the team used a multi-voting process with the decision-making as a shared action, thus resulting in a shared and agreed upon resolution.

Fourth Principle – Insist on Using Objective Criteria

According to Fisher and Ury, "the approach is to commit yourself to reaching a solution based on principle, not pressure. Concentrate on the merits of the problem, not the mettle of the parties. Be open to reason but closed to threats" (Fisher and Ury, 2011, p. 84). This last principle, which uses objective criteria, means that the negotiations should employ agreed-upon ground rules, accepted data, and facts. The objective criteria are the parameters to be established around the negotiation. They will create a fair environment in which to frame the procedures and acceptance criteria which will govern the negotiation. These criteria need to be generated by each party and presented with a rationale of why these criteria meet the standard of fairness. Some examples of objective criteria include having respect for one another and espousing honest communication, the timing of meetings, voting uses, and methods of providing data to all the parties. Fisher and Ury's (2011) principles of negotiation are widely used and, in this case, can be seen as part of the ethical leader's core values: individual respect and honesty in all relationships.

6.6.2 Thomas Kilmann Conflict Model

The **Thomas Kilmann Conflict Model (TKI)** from Kilmann Diagnostics narrows the focus of conflict resolution to the emotive characteristics of those involved and their specific approaches to conflict management. The model first identifies two dimensions of individual behavior when approaching a conflict situation: assertiveness and cooperativeness. Assertiveness refers to the need and extent of an individual's desire to meet their own needs and concerns. Cooperativeness represents the willingness of an individual to meet the needs and issues of others. The TKI model uses these two dimensions of individual behavior (assertiveness and cooperativeness) to define five different modes for responding to conflict situations: competing, collaborating, compromising, avoiding, and accommodating (figure 6.3).

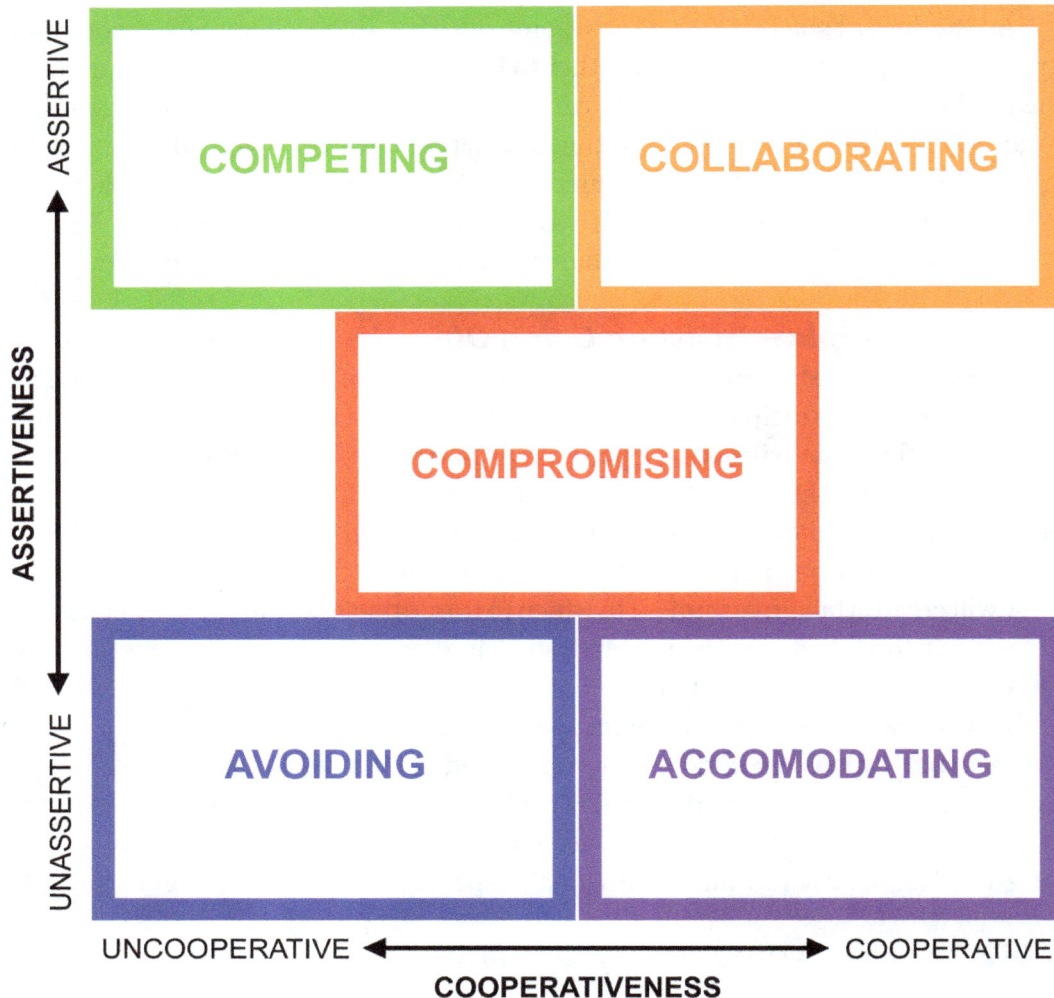

Figure 6.3: Thomas Kilmann Conflict Model
Source: Original Work
Attribution: Corey Parson, adapted from Challenging Coaching
License: Fair Use

Competing - Most uncooperative/assertive – This situation is the proverbial "win-lose" scenario of conflict. Such behavior demonstrates an unwillingness for both parties to consider any form of resolution. If we apply ethical leadership traits here, we see the authority/power paradigm as the dominant trait. Inclusion is missing as well as conscientious concern for the other party. It is a "win at all costs" mentality.

Accommodating – Most cooperative and least assertive – This dimension is the opposite of competing. Many adjectives can be used to describe the behavior of accommodating parties: self-sacrificing, generous, selfless, charitable, and yielding (TKI Overview, n.d.). Still, while this type of conflict negotiation may seem the "nice" way to go, it is not the most ethical. Keep in mind that ethical leaders are compelled by their personal values to "do the right thing" and "do no harm." Ethical leaders cannot just sacrifice their position to make others happy;

for instance, what are the conditions when an ethical leader can compromise the "do no harm" value?

Avoiding – Least cooperative and assertive – This mode is characterized by parties who demonstrate little to no regard for the outcome. Individuals operating in this mode refuse to acknowledge the existence of the conflict or work around it, demonstrating a passive-resistant behavior. The hope by a party taking this approach is that by ignoring the conflict, maybe it will gradually disappear (TKI Overview, n.d.). A truly ethical leader would not take this approach to negotiate conflict.

Collaboration - Most assertive and cooperative – This conflict management style is the proverbial "win-win" solution to any conflict. Both parties involved make it a point that the conflict solution "satisfies" each concern on at least a partial basis. As per our description of an ethical leader, it means a willingness to honestly listen and share all aspects of the conflict situation—even to the point of using the conflict to learn from each other as seen in an inclusive environment. The ethical collaboration fits well and can create trust and understanding beyond the solution of a single conflict (TKI Overview, n.d.).

Edmund Burke (1775)

> *All government—indeed every human benefit and enjoyment, every virtue and every prudent act—is founded on compromise and barter.*

Compromising – Moderately assertive and cooperative – As stated by the TKI Overview, "The objective is to find some expedient, mutually acceptable solution that partially satisfies both parties" (TKI Overview, n.d.). This dimension can be characterized as a "win-lose/win-lose" solution. Each party agrees that they will be partially satisfied with the solution. Because the decision does not bring closure the conflict may come back again, but it is a middle-ground concession by both parties. Ethical leadership behavior can both accept these terms and reject them on the principle of "do the right thing" and "do no harm." If the compromised solution is partially right and only doing a small amount of harm, can it be called an ethical solution? Is compromise ethically acceptable?

Compromise, while practical in execution, can indeed lead to ethical compromises, which posits an ethical dilemma. For example, this approach has been demonstrated many times in history. A classic compromise case is the Yalta Conference between the United States, the United Kingdom, and the Soviet Union attempting to create a post-war peace. Each had to sacrifice goals for lasting peace and settle for a mutual stalemate position.

In summary, as Thomas and Kilmann explain, "Each of us is capable of using all five conflict-handling modes. None of us can be characterized as having a single style of dealing with conflict. But certain people use some modes better than others and, therefore, tend to rely on those modes more heavily than others—whether because of temperament or practice." Therefore, individual behavior, when engaged in conflict, has a personal predisposition towards one of the previously discussed approaches. However, the situational dynamics of the conflict itself also places a demand on the individual party and may change their approach.

6.7 APPLICATION PROFILE

James Burke – Johnson and Johnson: The Tylenol Crisis

James Burke's ethical leadership became evident during the Tylenol Crisis his company Johnson & Johnson (J&J) faced in the fall of 1982. In 1982, seven people died after taking cyanide-laced extra-strength Tylenol capsules sold in five Chicago stores. Before then the product Tylenol, sold by J&J's McNeil Consumer Products division, had 35% of the $1.2 billion analgesic market. After the deaths, J&J's market share dropped to 7%. However, Burke took immediate action to have all the company's Tylenol capsules removed across the country, despite the fact that this decision created a large financial loss for the organization. Burke emphasized the value of the J&J credo, dating back to the company's founding in 1887, which stated that the company is responsible first to its customers, then to its employees, the community, and the stockholders, in that order. "The credo is all about the consumer," Burke said. When those seven deaths occurred, "the credo made it very clear at that point exactly what we were all about. It gave me the ammunition I needed to persuade shareholders and others to spend the $100 million on the recall. The credo helped sell it." He went even further than that. He allowed the media to follow company meetings, he spoke on several occasions on TV and he introduced new protections to the way the organization packaged its products. The costs were not added to the price but were absorbed by the organization. Burke saved not only the reputation of the company, but also the brand. By mid-1983, Tylenol's share of the analgesic market had climbed to 30%, reaching 35% by the end of the year.

James Burke received the Presidential Medal of Freedom in 2000 and was named one of history's 10 greatest CEOs by Fortune magazine in 2003. But it was for his handling of the Tylenol tragedy back in 1982 that Burke, CEO of Johnson & Johnson from 1976 to 1989, will be remembered most. In an interview for a 2004 book *Lasting Leadership*, Burke said, "You tell me any human relationship that works without trust, whether it is a marriage or a friendship or a social interaction; in the long run, the same thing is true about business."

6.8 SUMMARY

In this chapter we looked at leadership ethics both generally and specifically by addressing organizational conflict and ethical leadership. In this discussion, the ethical attributes of character and actions (behavior) were both addressed as key elements in the evaluation of leadership ethics. Other attributes included goals of honesty, power, and values. The chapter addressed ethical leadership attributes, concluding with the statement that the origins of leadership ethics begin with a leader's personal values. Personal ethical values define a leader's character and ultimately lead to ethical behavior. This chapter made an overarching conclusion that there is no such thing as specific ethical behavior for particular domains, such as business, politics, etc. Ethics and ethical behavior, regardless of the domain, are based solely on personal values and character; the environment is a secondary factor that triggers leaders' values and actions. This concept was demonstrated in various examples of ethical leadership, and was especially pronounced in decision-making scenarios.

The chapter also addressed the challenges of ethical leadership by discussing the subject of how a good leader uses ethical principles to manage conflict in the organization. It pointed out that conflict is between at least two parties over any intangible or tangible subject/object. Fundamentally, per Walzlawick, et. al (1967), communication, both content and relational, or a lack thereof between the two parties is what leads to conflict. The chapter then addressed how conflict can be managed based on the theory of principled negotiation by Fisher and Ury (2011), which we used as a strategy for ethical leaders. It also discussed various leadership behavioral styles by Kilmann and Thomas (1977), explaining how ethical leadership may adopt some of these styles to mitigate organizational conflict. Using this comparison of ethical leadership styles and various conflict resolution strategies completed the discussion of ethical leadership and conflict resolution.

Chapter 7 will also address obstacles, not just to ethical but also to effective leadership. Some of the obstacles this next chapter will look at are clarifying goals, facing apathy in the organization, providing positive feedback, simplifying complex tasks, and creating rewarding challenges for routine tasks. It will present various techniques and methods, such as different types of leadership, that supervisors can use to eliminate obstacles in their staff's performance and overall organization. Indeed, chapter 7 is a companion to this chapter in relation to conflict resolution.

6.9 DISCUSSION QUESTIONS

1. Construct a working definition of leadership ethics.
2. Discuss the nature of the conflict environment.
3. What are the key practices in ethical leadership to manage conflict?
4. Discuss the concept of negotiation in conflict resolution.
5. What is the impact of ethical and unethical leadership in managing organizational conflict?

6.10 FURTHER READING

Aspira Continuing Education. 2010. "Conflict Resolution." https://aspirace.com/wp-content/uploads/2015/11/Conflict_Resolution_CEU_Continuing_Education_Course.pdf.

BBC. n.d. "Ethics: Introduction to Ethics." http://www.bbc.co.uk/ethics/introduction/.

Bennis, Warren 1994. An Invented Life: Reflections on Leadership and Change. New York: Perseus Books Group.

Costa, P. T., & McCrae, R. R. (1992). Revised NEO personality inventory: NEO PI and NEO five-factor inventory (NEO FFI professional manual). Odessa, FL: Psychological Assessment Resources.

Cleverism. 2016. "Ethical Leadership Guide: Definition, Qualities, Pros & Cons, Example." May, 2016. https://www.cleverism.com/ethical-leadership-guide-definition-qualities-pros-cons-examples/.

Fact Sheet, Wilson Learning, n.d. Accessed December 20, 2019 from https://www.wilsonlearning.com/documents/factsheets/en/FS_NegotiatingToYes_Corporate_16_en.pdf.

Menkel-Medows, Carrie. Ethics of Compromise. Found in A. Farazmand (ed.), Global Encyclopedia of Public Administration, Public Policy, and Governance, 2016. Springer International Publishing, Accessed December 21, 2019, from https://www.law.uci.edu/faculty/full-time/menkel-meadow/ethics-as-compromise-Ency.of-Public-Admin-and-Policy.pdf.

Moriarty, Jeffrey, "Business Ethics", The Stanford Encyclopedia of Philosophy (Fall 2017 Edition), Edward N. Zalta (ed.). Accessed on December 19, 2019 from URL = <https://plato.stanford.edu/archives/fall2017/entries/ethics-business/>.

Putnam, L. L. (2010). Communication as changing the negotiation game. Journal of Applied Communication Research, 38(4), 325– 335.

Whitbeck, Joanne. Unit 4: Do Certain personality traits create ethical leaders?. PennState Liberal Arts Online. 2017. Accessed December 19, 2019 from https://sites.psu.edu/psy533wheeler/2017/03/23/unit-4-are-certain-personalities-more-ethical/.

6.11 REFERENCES

Brown, Michael E. and Trevino, Linda K. 2006. "Ethical leadership: A review and future directions". The Leadership Quarterly 17, 595-616. Accessed November 30, 2019. https://www.mcgill.ca/engage/files/engage/ethical_leadership_2006.pdf.

Challenging Coaching. 2013 Kilmann, Ralph. H. Conflict and Challenge. Access December 2, 2019 https://challengingcoaching.co.uk/conflict-and-challenge/.

Dillon, Bernadette and Bourke, Juliet. 2016. "6 Characteristics of Inclusive Leaders". CIO Journal, May 4, 2016. Accessed December 5,2019. https://deloitte.wsj.com/cio/2016/05/04/6-characteristics-of-inclusive-leaders/.

Fisher, Roger and Ury, William. 2011. *Getting to yes: Negotiating agreement without giving in, 3rd ed.* New York, NY: Penguin Books.

Fisher, Roger and Ury, William. "Principled Negotiation – The Harvard Approach.". n.d. Accessed December 5, 2019. *https://www.eiseverywhere.com/file_uploads/ fd90f7b5575b6d9229dfb17bf132b299_ER2017_CollaboratingwithSchools_ SandyMislow_Handout-PrincipledNegotiation.pdf.*

French, John R. P. and Raven, Bertram. 1959. "The bases of social power". *In Studies in Social Power,* edited by D. Cartwright, 150-167. University of Michigan. Accessed November 30, 2019. https://www.researchgate.net/publication/215915730_The_ bases_of_social_power/link/02bfe50d2462a9e0c8000000/download.

Hocker, Joyce L.and Wilmot, William. 2010. *Interpersonal Conflict.* United Kingdom: McGraw-Hill.

Kalshoven, K., Den Hartog, D.N. and De Hoogh, A.H.B. 2010. 2011. "Ethical Leader Behavior and Big Five Factors of Personality." *Journal of Business Ethics,* 100, 349–366. doi:10.1007/s10551-010-0685-9.

Kilmann, Ralph. H., and Thomas, Kenneth. W. 1977. *Developing a forced-choice measure of conflict handling behavior: The "mode" instrument.* n.d. Accessed December 1, 2019 https://www.researchgate.net/profile/Ralph_Kilmann/ publication/247726333_Developing_a_Forced-Choice_Measure_of_Conflict- Handling_Behavior_The_Mode_Instrument/links/0a85e539b118b87348000000/ Developing-a-Forced-Choice-Measure-of-Conflict-Handling-Behavior-The-Mode- Instrument.pdf.

Kilmann Diagnostics. n.d. Kilmann, Ralph. H., and Thomas, Kenneth. W. *OVERVIEW OF THE THOMAS-KILMANN CONFLICT MODE INSTRUMENT (TKI)..* Access December 1, 2019. https://kilmanndiagnostics.com/overview-thomas-kilmann- conflict-mode-instrument-tki/.

Maxwell, John. 2003. *Ethics 101: What every leader needs to know.* New York, NY: Center Street.

Messick, David M. and Bazerman, Max H. 1996. "Ethical leadership and the psychology of decision making", *MIT Sloan Management Review,* Winter 1996. Accessed November 30, 2019 https://sloanreview.mit.edu/article/ethical-leadership-and-the- psychology-of-decision-making/.

Northouse, Peter G. 2018. Introduction to Leadership: Concepts and Practice, in 4th ed. Thousand Oaks, CA: Sage Publications Inc.

Subhasree, K. 2010. "Ethical Leadership: Best Practice for Success." *Journal of Business and Management [online],* 22 (7), 112-116. http://www.iosrjournals.org/iosr-jbm/ papers/ICIMS/Volume-1/14.pdf> [18 September 2017].

Watzlawick, Paul. Bevin, Janet. D. Jackson Donald. 1967. *Pragmatics of Human Communication. A study of interactional patterns, pathologies, and paradoxes.* New York and London: WW Norton & Co.

Weinstein, Bruce. "Seven Bold Leaders Reveal How Ethical Leadership is a Boon to Business", *Forbes*, Oct 14, 2019. https://www.forbes.com/sites/bruceweinstein/2019/10/14/seven-bold-leaders-reveal-how-ethical-leadership-is-a-boon-to-business/#781debc8454c.

7 Surmounting Obstacles to Effective Leadership

7.1 LEARNING OBJECTIVES

After reading this chapter, students will be able to

1. Describe obstacles to effective leadership

2. Compare the types of obstacles to effective leadership

3. Assess different leadership styles and techniques intended to respond to these obstacles

7.2 KEY TERMS

- Obstacles
- Directive leadership
- Supportive leadership
- Participatory leadership
- Achievement oriented leadership

7.3 INTRODUCTION

In the previous chapter, we examined the ethics of leadership, demonstrating that ethics are personal rather than organizational. In this chapter, we turn from internal ethical struggles and look at other issues that can create barriers to success. Everyone encounters struggles, every family, every person, every leader, and every organization. One task of a good leader is to anticipate barriers and assist their team in overcoming them. The idea of a leader assisting their team in overcoming obstacles comes out of a theory called Path-Goal Leadership (House, 1971, 1996), which concentrates on the ways that leaders can create an environment where teams detect and overcome obstacles effectively. Based on House's concept (1996), good leaders can assist their teams in overcoming **obstacles** to reach their goals effectively (see figure 7.1). The most successful leaders forge new pathways around obstacles through ideas and innovation, while maintaining the ethics, values, and mission of the organization. In this chapter, we discuss seven of the most common obstacles leaders and their teams will encounter and some leadership types and techniques available to navigating through and around such problems to achieve organizational objectives.

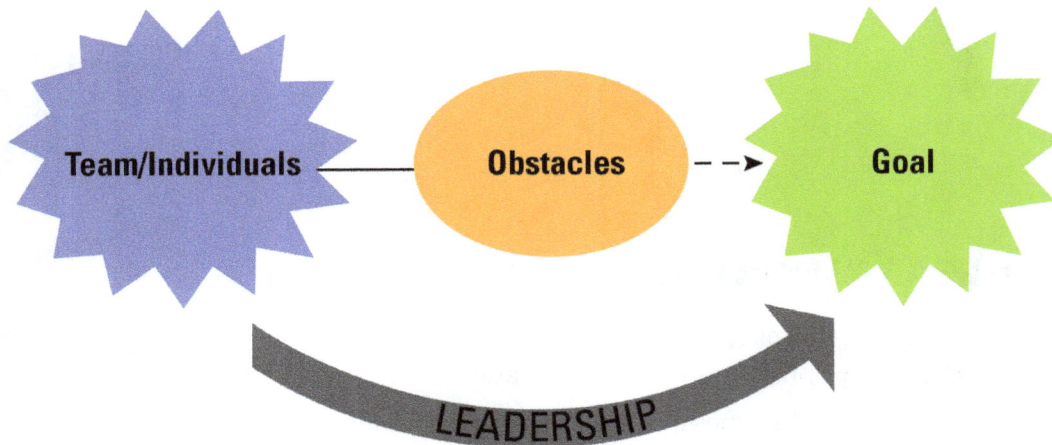

Figure 7.1: Overcoming Obstacles
Source: Original Work
Attribution: Heather Mbaye
License: CC BY-SA 4.0

7.4 THE OBSTACLES

Following House (1971), best practices recognize 7 distinct obstacles teams face that effective leadership can overcome. These are:

1. indistinct goals
2. indefinite direction
3. apathy
4. multifaceted tasks
5. repetitive tasks
6. detachment, and
7. routine.

In this section, we will review each of these hurdles individually and examine ways to overcome them.

7.5 INDISTINCT GOALS

People and organizations are more likely to work towards understanding, agreeing upon, and achieving specific, rather than general, goals. General goals can be too easy to redefine and ultimately not reach, so they should be clear and understandable thereby enabling teams to achieve them. For example, if your goal is to "get good grades in college," you will need to answer the question, what do "good grades" really mean? If the answer is too general, then you could alter your definition of "good grades" according to the grades you are receiving. A more specific, and therefore more workable, goal would be "achieve a GPA of at least 3.3 in college," or "get all As and Bs in college."

Leaders therefore must set clear, achievable goals. If the goal is too vague, such as "produce more widgets," then the team does not know what exactly it is working to accomplish, nor does the leader have a way to measure whether or not the team has accomplished the desired task. A more specific goal would ask the team to produce 1000 widgets per day. Each person may define "more" differently. Would one more per day be enough? 10? 100? Specifics, like 1000 widgets per day, will prevent confusion: everyone knows what "1000 additional widgets" means. Without such specific, measurable goals, teams can become frustrated and discouraged because leaders and teams alike don't know if they are achieving their goals.

Similarly, teams may sometimes face multiple and competing goals. In that circumstance, leaders must not only make sure the goals are specific and measurable but also make clear their priorities—and rank the goals, if necessary.

7.5.1 Examples of Clear Goals

Here are some examples of clear, specific, and measurable goals:
- A volunteer organization providing meals to the homeless: Reduce the outlay cost of meals from $5 each to $4.50 each without reducing the amount or quality of food. This goal would replace "reduce costs."

- State highway patrol: Reduce the number of traffic fatalities by increasing seatbelt use through targeted advertisements and ticketing campaigns. This goal would replace "improve highway safety."

- A garment manufacturer: Find a less expensive supplier of buttons to reduce button cost by 10% across the board. This goal would replace "reduce costs."

- Basketball coach: Improve three-point percentage from 28% to 30% across all team-members. This goal would replace "win more games."

Goals, as discussed in this section, should be SMART; that is, they should be **S**pecific, **M**easurable, **A**chievable, **R**elevant, and **T**ime bound (they should not be open-ended but should have a deadline) (Bogue, 2018, Doran, 1981). This concept is used by many organizations and effective leaders.

7.6 INDEFINITE DIRECTIONS

Have you ever tried to assemble a Lego™ set without the instructions? You may have a set that should look like the White House but end up with just a white house, and a lot of leftover bricks. This conundrum represents what can happen when directions are absent in the workplace. Vague instructions may be as equally damaging as absent ones. For example, what if you only have the directions in a language you can't read, so you're trying to go by the photos alone? Bad or no directions will lead to inefficiencies and failures in a team.

Leaders therefore must provide clear, detailed, and unequivocal directions to reaching a goal. Sometimes, even with a clear goal, employees are not sure how to proceed. Suppose your professor gives you a topic, and then says, "write a paper." How do you proceed when you're missing specifics, like length, whether or not it should be an opinion piece, if you should be doing a literature review, due date, etc.? What does your professor want in order for you to reach your goal of earning an A on that essay? Students will be more successful if they have the answers to such questions as these. Similarly, employees need the answers to their questions in order to achieve organizational objectives.

The best leaders give clear directions at the correct level and help individual team members find a path to the group's goals. After all, not every employee requires the same degree of direction. What one employee may find helpful, another may consider micromanaging. Leaders must use their social skills to determine team members' needs and adapt to those needs. Leaders should be aware, for instance, that some people, including students, need more specifics, while others want to be told the ultimate goal and given general outlines so they may proceed on their own.

7.7 APATHY

Lack of motivation yields a lack of productivity. Clearly, a leader cannot force motivation. If an employee simply does not want to work, even the best leader cannot make them do so. Nonetheless, a good leader strives to avoid apathy by setting goals that everyone can believe in; if people value what they do, they will be more motivated to do it. Goals must not only be inspiring, but employees also need to see that their efforts are paying off. In other words, people need to see that what they are being asked to do will in fact advance the team on the path to their goal. Being able to achieve such significant results prevents one from considering their tasks as merely "busy work." One of the most important tasks of a good leader is motivating employees to perform at a high level. Sometimes this task requires creating an incentive, that is, a carrot; other times, this duty requires introducing a threat of punishment, that is, a stick. Typically, incentives work better for most people, with punishment being a last resort.

Incentives that leaders can use to combat apathy include rewards and positive feedback. Motivations like bonuses help maintain employee drive as long as the rewards are specific and there is follow through. Sometimes it's advantageous to give individuals bonuses. If a company sets a goal to increase sales by 25%, they might reasonably expect to give salespeople bonuses for meeting or exceeding that goal. Companies should make clear what the expected reward will be. Importantly, leaders should not change the goal midway. That is to say, if a leader sets a bonus to pay out at a 25% increase in sales in a year, they should not change the rate to 35% midway through the year. Any promised rewards *must* be granted upon goal achievement; otherwise, apathy will increase.

Similarly, positive feedback helps everyone feel competent and therefore more motivated to accomplish team goals. For example, when one team leader was away on vacation, their team sold an order netting the company $100,000. When they returned, instead of praising the team for this major order, the boss pointed out they could have made $102,500 if they'd used a different part number from a different supplier. This response frustrated and irritated the whole team, whose justifiable pride in the large sale was deflated by their boss's reaction. This sort of guidance on improvement would be fine if the boss had first celebrated the team's positive outcomes. Such reactions lacking positive reinforcement breed apathy. Team members likely will ask themselves, why bother putting together major orders on top of their other work when their boss won't appreciate it anyway? It would have been far more effective if the leader had instead called for a lunch delivery to celebrate the sale, and, later—perhaps several weeks later—pointed out the alternate supplier for next time.

7.8 MULTIFACETED TASKS

Some tasks are very complicated so can seem overwhelming. When goals are complex, an effective leader will combat confusion and frustration by breaking tasks down into smaller goals to be reached along the way. They will, in effect, set milestones along the pathway to the goal. This strategy is called **directive leadership**, which entails giving specific directions, intermediate goals, and timelines where needed. For instance, if your personal goal is to earn a cumulative 3.3 GPA in school, you may set interim goals, such as achieving all As and Bs each semester. Indeed, you might even break the goal down further into grade goals for each test, or by setting study times for each class. These intermediate and short-term goals bring the long-term goal—the cumulative GPA—to life through gradual accomplishments. A good leader will help you set these short- and medium-term goals in order to reach the primary, and otherwise complex, goal.

In a similar vein, some employees have multiple, coinciding goals so may struggle with prioritization. For example, a sales associate may find it difficult to prioritize and focus when the phone is ringing and every call is an emergency. Whether facing constant interruptions or competing customers, some people need help managing their workload by setting rules to determine which goals they should prioritize.

Similarly, some employees may find it difficult to not only prioritize but also manage multiple, equally important tasks to completion without distraction and interruptions. In such circumstances, a good leader helps the employee break the multiple goals into manageable intermediate ones. Additionally, they will encourage the employee to set boundaries on outside interruptions; doing so will help the employee focus on finishing more important tasks first.

7.9 REPETITIVE TASKS

Repetitive and simple tasks, though often necessary in any workplace, can become boring and create dissatisfaction for individuals on the team. Without an exciting challenge, some people find completing tasks difficult. This obstacle requires **supportive leadership**, which involves bringing an encouraging, humanizing aspect to boring, repetitive jobs. In every workplace or team situation, some employees regularly work on boring, rote, and repetitive tasks. To counter this situation, a leader may need to bolster the employees' spirits with praise and empathy. It is important to demonstrate real interest in an employee's work, even when it's not particularly creative. The personal touch can help employees stay motivated through the tiresome parts of a project and get through to more interesting tasks.

7.10 DETACHMENT

It is possible to be too emotionally invested in your job, that is, to have so much emotional investment in it that it is difficult to accept constructive feedback. However, the reverse is also certainly true: it is possible to be too detached. Some level of emotional investment in your job creates motivation to produce the best possible work. Individuals who feel too detached from their work or organization, though, may fail in productivity and instead work only to accomplish the bare minimum. One way to combat detachment— and create buy-in among team members— is to let employees know that leaders value their input in decisions and consider it important. If employees don't feel heard, they become detached. For example, it is the responsibility of a university department chair to look at enrollments and decide which classes are needed. If the chair decides unilaterally which classes each professor will teach and at what times, the faculty members may resent not being consulted and consequently feel discontented. **Participatory leaders** are those who include their teams in their decision making and make an effort to hear each person's voice. A participatory department chair, for example, will include faculty members in the decision-making process, asking them which classes they want to teach and when, so that everyone's needs are considered. It may not be possible for the leader to satisfy all constituents completely, but the process of being heard and attempting to listen and satisfy is a crucial step in combatting organizational and team detachment. A participatory leader is *democratic*, requesting team and individual input and feedback, being responsive and friendly, and remaining open-minded to change and ideas from team members. Democratic participatory leaders have the best chance to avoid detachment in their employees by including them in the process of decision making and giving them a stake in the final outcome.

7.11 ROUTINE

While repetitive tasks pose obstacles to some employees, unaltered routines may pose obstacles to other employees who find such routines to be uninteresting. Such team members, who are craving challenge, will find themselves "phoning it in," that is, doing the bare minimum. **Achievement oriented** leadership seeks to eliminate this barrier to productivity by creating a challenge for all employees to do the best they can. Achievement oriented leaders will create challenges from the routine, and will create opportunities for achievement even within routine tasks. In situations where the work is routine, for example, these leaders will give "gold stars" to their team; they will make the challenge earning the bonus, the A+, the extra credit, rather than the work itself. As a student, I found myself in a summer job in a county tax office in which I did a lot of filing in old fashioned filing cabinets. It was exacting, had to be done correctly, and was very routine. I was faced each day with filing not only the whole office's previous day's work but also with completing a little bit of the filing backlog. For me, the challenge was to get through the backlog so I could learn the more interesting parts of the job. By the end of the summer, all the backlog was complete so I was moved to more interesting tasks. A good leader will see what each person needs in order to be motivated to do their best.

7.12 SUMMARY

Overcoming obstacles requires the use of different leadership styles, tactics, and combinations thereof. It also depends upon the specific employees involved as well as the organization's values, mission, and objectives. This chapter has reviewed 7 types of obstacles to effective leadership and ways to overcome them.

First, goals should be clear and measurable so that teams and leaders can achieve them. Similarly, because indefinite directions will lead to team inefficiencies and failures, leaders should provide clear, detailed, and unequivocal directions to reaching a goal. Lack of motivation, or apathy, yields a lack of productivity. A good leader strives to avoid apathy by setting goals that everyone can believe in. If people value what they do, they will be more motivated to do it. Likewise, positive feedback helps everyone feel competent and therefore more motivated to accomplish team goals.

Some multifaceted tasks are very complicated so can seem overwhelming. Leaders may break such tasks down into smaller goals to be reached along the way. This strategy is called **directive leadership**, which entails giving specific directions, intermediate goals, and timelines where needed. Likewise, repetitive and simple tasks, though often necessary in any workplace, can become boring and create dissatisfaction for individuals on the team. Without an exciting challenge, some people find completing tasks difficult. This obstacle requires **supportive leadership**, which involves bringing an encouraging, humanizing aspect to boring, repetitious jobs. The obstacle of detachment can lead to low productivity. **Participatory leaders** are those who include their teams in their decision making to encourage emotional attachment. Finally, routine tasks can pose an obstacle to those who crave challenge. **Achievement oriented** leadership seeks to eliminate this barrier to productivity by creating a challenge for all employees to do the best they can.

In the next chapter, the book turns to the practical application of effective leadership. A leader's primary task is to motivate their team to do better. Effective leadership can increase employee motivation by providing variety, identity, significance, autonomy, and feedback.

7.13 DISCUSSION QUESTIONS

1. What are the 7 main types of obstacles?

2. Can you think of specific examples from your own school and work life regarding the problem of indistinct goals? What was the indistinct goal, and how could it have been changed and made clearer?

3. Under what circumstances would the elimination of one of these obstacles for some team members create new obstacles for those team members or for others?

4. Which type of leadership—directive, supportive, participatory, or achievement-oriented—would you say you're better at than others? In which area do you need the most work? How would you go about improving your leadership in that category?

7.14 FURTHER READING

Bridges, Jennifer (2020). "Common Leadership Challenges." https://www. projectmanager.com/training/leadership-challenges.

Brodie, Duncan (2020). "7 Obstacles to Effective Leadership" https:// goalsandachievements.com/7-obstacles-to-effective-leadership/.

7.15 REFERENCES

Bogue, Robert. "Use S.M.A.R.T. goals to launch management by objectives plan". TechRepublic. Retrieved 10 February 2018.

Doran, G. T. (1981). "There's a S.M.A.R.T. way to write management's goals and objectives". Management Review. 70 (11): 35–36.

House, Robert J. 1996. "Path-Goal Theory of Leadership: Lessons, Legacy, and a Reformulated Theory." Leadership Quarterly 7 (3): 323.

House, Robert J., and Ram N. Aditya. "The Social Scientific Study of Leadership: Quo Vadis?" Journal of Management 23, no. 3 (June 1997): 409–73.

Schriesheim, C. A., & DeNisi, A. S. (1981). Task dimensions as moderators of the effects of instrumental leadership: A two-sample replicated test of path–goal leadership theory. Journal of Applied Psychology, 66(5), 589–597.

8 Putting it All Together— Making Leadership Work For You

8.1 LEARNING OBJECTIVES

After reading this chapter, students will

1. Understand the concept of situational leadership

2. Understand the characteristics of effective leaders

3. Recognize how different leaders and leadership techniques affect followers

4. Understand how leadership affects followers outside of the confines of the workplace

8.2 KEY TERMS

- Situational Leadership
- Authoritarian Leadership
- Job Burnout
- Engagement
- Structural Frame
- Human Resource Frame
- Political Frame
- Symbolic Frame

8.3 INTRODUCTION

This book so far has introduced theories of leadership, leadership styles, and organizational challenges to leadership. Previous chapters have discussed creating vision and mission statements as well as the skills needed to lead and manage diverse organizations. We have considered the importance of ethical leadership and how to overcome potential obstacles and barriers to achieving both individual and organizational goals. This final chapter, then, answers the ultimate question of significance: "so what?" In answer, this chapter will focus on the practical application of leadership and how effective leadership is critical to an organization's success. The chapter additionally will examine some real-world case studies of effective leaders in order to better illustrate the implementation of leadership skills to which you have been introduced in this textbook.

Effective leadership can increase the motivation of your stakeholders and create organizational cohesiveness. Colquitt and Piccolo (2006) suggest individuals are more likely to become self-motivated if their work provides the following:

- "variety"— jobs that require using a number of skills and talents
- "identity"— jobs that allow completion of a "whole" piece of work, or doing a task from start to finish with a definite outcome
- "significance"— jobs that have an impact on the lives of other people
- "autonomy"— jobs that provide reasonable freedom and encourage independent thought, and
- "feedback"— clear information about performance levels (p. 329).

8.4 SITUATIONAL LEADERSHIP

Again, the previous chapters of this book reviewed many ways by which individuals can become "good" leaders. However, to synthesize this information, we shall shift from thinking about what makes someone a "good" leader to what makes someone an "effective" leader. "Good" is a largely subjective term and varies from person to person and organization to organization. Effectiveness, on the other hand, allows us to examine the traits that allow leaders to achieve organizational success regardless of the particular methodology they use or their organizational contexts. Effectiveness affords us the opportunity to discuss one of the most important contextual factors related to leadership, that leadership is largely situational.

Situational leadership is predicated on the idea that effective leadership is about not only the *who* but also, largely, the *when*. This concept holds that some leaders are more effective in certain situations and within certain contexts. In times of crisis, when decisive action is necessary to keep people safe or to keep the organization afloat, the most effective leader may have **authoritarian** tendencies. These types of leaders tend to dictate policies and procedures to the institution. Input from followers is non-existent (or kept to a minimum), and most of the organizational communication comes from a singular leader. During crises, this style may be the most effective method to guide the organization. If it is critical to speak in one voice, with one message, then using a singular leader who speaks on behalf of the organization is likely the right call. However, if things were going well and the organization was looking to push beyond its current capabilities, they may more effectively be led by someone who is inclusive, allows for the reciprocal flow of information and encourages feedback and constructive criticism. A leader who exudes optimism and promotes an inclusive workplace community may be more effective in this scenario. Clearly, effective leadership isn't always simply about being the right person for the job. Rather, it is about whether or not you are the right person for the job at that particular moment in time with that particular group of people (or the right person for what the organization is hoping to be).

8.5 WHY EFFECTIVE LEADERSHIP MATTERS

The influence of leaders on an organization goes beyond the walls of the workplace. While it is no surprise that a leader's effectiveness directly correlates to the organization's productivity, people often forget that effective leadership also affects many other aspects of the organization. Truly effective organizations have to be mindful of the fact that individuals within the workspace do not exist within a vacuum. They are more than the work they do. They have families, as well as external obligations and pressures that may have nothing to do with the goals of the organization (and, in some circumstances, may run counter to the goals of the organization).

Therefore, the organizational environment and culture, set in part by the leader, affects the outside lives of employees in ways that may affect their performance. Borrill, et. al (2004), examine this impact of leaders, noting the positive correlation between supportive leadership styles and subordinate self-esteem. They find that subordinate behavior may affect the leader's perception of their employees, thus resulting in possible negative treatment from supervisors. Subordinates who display negative attitudes and appear depressed or anxious may suffer worse treatment from supervisors. Individuals by nature prefer people who are pleasant, so managers may inadvertently avoid subordinates who display such negative behaviors. The authors identify this phenomenon as a *loss spiral*, which exists when an increase in negative feelings among subordinates leads to a decrease in supportive leadership behavior and vice versa (Borrill, et. al, 2004, p. 173). It becomes imperative, then, that effective leaders practice empathy and recognize that their behavior has an impact, again, on the way people live their lives outside of work. Below are some ways that leadership affects people outside of the organizational context.

8.5.1 Leadership affects Physical Wellbeing

Research indicates that leaders play a critical role in improving employee well-being by reducing emotional exhaustion. Emotional exhaustion is a key indicator of burnout, a phenomenon experienced by approximately 77% of employees in the U.S. The Mayo Clinic defines **job burnout** as "a state of physical or emotional exhaustion that also involves a sense of reduced accomplishment and loss of personal identity." Its physical symptoms include insomnia, headaches, chest pains, and shortness of breath. Some studies have even linked burnout to issues such as anxiety and depression. Effective leaders are mindful of the physical well-being of their followers. Effective leaders will work to create an environment that focuses on the employee experience in support of their well-being. Research notes that employees who experience exhaustion are less likely to feel connected and committed to the organization and are more likely to quit. Therefore, the most effective leaders work against such outcomes by promoting a healthy work-life balance for their employees.

8.5.2 Leadership affects Mental Health

Benson and Gilbreath found that "employees working for a supervisor who was perceived to frequently engage in positive behaviors and rarely in negative behaviors reported having much better psychological health. There is a substantial research base indicating that supervision can effect employee well-being" (Benson & Gilbreath, 2004, p. 264). Stressful work events including anxiety, burnout, and depression also have a negative impact on employees' mental health. In fact, research by Bupa Global (an international health insurer) found that 64% of senior business leaders have suffered from mental health conditions, with a majority citing work as the significant contributing factor. Mental Health America notes that depression costs over $43,000,000,000 in absenteeism, lost productivity, and direct treatment expenses. In 2019, the World Health Organization in fact noted that depression and anxiety cost the U.S. economy approximately one trillion dollars. Effective leaders, then, realize that mental health directly relates to their organization's productivity levels. In fact, the WHO offers that every $1.00 the U.S. puts into increased treatment for common mental disorders has a return of $4.00 in improved health and productivity. Considering how much of one's life is spent at work, the most effective leaders make mental health a priority in their organizations.

8.5.3 Leadership affects Engagement

We have noted in this text that effective leadership can increase employee motivation and make them more engaged in their work. Ineffective leadership can do the opposite. It is easy to confuse engagement with happiness—or the dreaded, but amorphous workplace satisfaction— but these terms are not interchangeable. Think about it like this: an employee might really like their organization's paid time off policy or be extremely happy with its generous health benefits. However, none of these things necessarily means that the employee is actually engaged with the work they are doing for their organization. Though definitions of **engagement** differ based on the organization, broadly speaking, engagement generally refers to the emotional connection and commitment an individual has to the organization. The following statistics illustrate the need for engagement to be a specific focus for an effective leader:

- According to the Engagement Institute, low employee engagement costs companies around the world between 450 to 550 billion dollars per year.

- According to Gallup, companies with a highly engaged workforce are 21% more profitable.

- According to O.C. Tanner's 2020 "Global Culture Report," 37% of employees consider recognition as the most important component of their engagement.

These statistics indicate that in order to keep the employees engaged, effective leaders have to recognize their employees' accomplishments. When they feel recognized, they are much more likely to feel a sense of pride connected to their work and a sense of loyalty and commitment to the organization. Effective leaders, therefore, recognize the importance of creating and taking advantage of opportunities to engage their followers.

8.6 THE RESPONSIBILITY OF LEADERSHIP: DO AS I SAY AND AS I DO

Leadership behaviors echo throughout an organization. Effective and ineffective leaders leave an indelible mark upon the organizations they represent. "The Contagious Leader: Impact of the Leader's Mood on the Mood of Group Members, Group Effective Tone, and Group Process" discusses the impact of leaders' "moods" on an organization. It was determined that leaders transfer their moods to other group members and mood can be "contagious" in an organization. This effect would be true for positive as well as negative moods. The implication of leader mood on an organization is significant because of the great power it holds over employees and their job performance.

This statement is a complicated way of saying that everything a leader does reverberate and has an impact on the organization. It isn't just what the leader says; it's also how they say it. It isn't just what the leader does; it is how they do it. Every action, or inaction, sends a message to employees about the things their boss values. Establishing a vision is important, but if the leader doesn't actually manifest that vision in the way they as the leader approach their work, then their words will ring hollow. If the leader espouses that their organization has a family atmosphere and collective decision making is important, yet they are insular in their decision making, the employee culture will suffer. Leadership isn't just about talking the talk; you have to walk the walk.

8.7 UNDERSTANDING YOUR ORGANIZATION: A SOCIAL SCIENCE APPROACH

The past forty years have seen an increased focus on the importance of understanding how organizations work and the characteristics the most successful organizations possess. Bolman and Deal (1984) attempted to consolidate various approaches to understanding organizations—specifically through a social science focused lens—and they introduced four frames through which to better understand how organizations, as well as the people who exist within those organizations, operate successfully. They argue that to be a truly effective leader requires understanding the intimate details of the organization. Their four frames, or lenses, through which the most effective leaders should understand their organizations are metaphors that encapsulate the broad areas of understanding critical importance within the organization. Bolman and Deal (2017) assert that organizations can be viewed through the following frames:

- **Structural Frame**: This frame imagines organizations as factories. Understanding this particular frame requires an in-depth understanding of the organization's inner workings, its systems, processes, technology, etc. Understanding the structures within the organization is critically important in order for a leader to operate at peak effectiveness.

- **Human Resource Frame**. This frame imagines organizations as families. It argues that effective leaders must understand the interpersonal relationships that exist both inside and outside the organization. The most effective leaders are able to recognize, and address, the needs of the members within their organizations. Trust is essential within this frame. This frame posits the simple mantra that happy employees tend to be more productive employees.

- **Political Frame**: This frame imagines organizations as jungles. It argues that, like a jungle, organizations are about power and that conflict is inevitable. As such, effective leaders understand the conflict and power dynamics within the organization and are able to leverage those politics into positive outcomes for the organization. Therefore, the more politically deft the leader of the organization is, the more effective the organization will be.

- **Symbolic Frame**: This frame imagines organizations as temples and carnivals. This frame argues that organizations are driven by symbols and culture. Developing a positive culture and understanding and utilizing symbols can help a leader gain a deeper understanding of the organization. Understanding the symbolism and background of an organization's culture enables a deeper appreciation of the context surrounding company and individual actions.

These frames are important, not because they are the only way to view an organization, but rather because they provide several different ways to examine it. These frames provide another set of tools for an effective leader. The idea is that by understanding all of the frames and thinking of them as a process, effective leaders will be able to gain a deeper understanding of the organization's component parts.

Information, then, is helpful when developing quality leadership. Remember, these frames are not a leadership style; rather, they are a way of thinking about and better understanding leadership. These frames will allow the most successful leaders to more deeply understand their organizations, thus making the leaders more effective.

8.8 PUTTING IT ALL TOGETHER

This book has examined theories of leadership as well as leadership philosophies and styles. We have discussed the importance of organizational vision, how to navigate leadership in diverse environments, and the importance of ethical leadership. We have spent time exploring how to overcome obstacles that individuals will face as leaders. Throughout all of these discussions, the hope is that readers recognize there is no "one-size-fits-all" model of leadership. Leaders operate differently depending on the organizations that they represent. Their behaviors and actions are affected by their followers and external stakeholders. Though the particular theory that a leader subscribes to may vary, effective leaders are able to leverage their strengths in order to move the organization beyond what it believed possible. The specifics of how an effective leader leads an organization will differ, but the underlying principles tend to remain the same.

In order to illustrate this quality, that effective leadership can come from a variety of leadership styles and perspectives, this chapter will now explore the undergirding principles of leadership and offer a brief leadership profile. Note that while the stylistic elements of leadership will change, each of the leaders discussed here were able to leverage their strengths and philosophies to motivate their followers and ultimately move their organizations toward achieving their goals. Though much literature focuses on what makes "good" leaders, our focus is on what makes a particular leader effective—keeping in mind that "good" leadership is subjective and situational, but effective leaders tend to have commonalities regardless of organizational type and culture.

8.8.1 Effective leaders rely on optimism

Leadership is an action that requires a destination and followers. Chapter one explores the evolution of leadership theory throughout history through a variety of lenses. All leaders, whether priests, poets, scholars, or kings, share a common trait of *influence*. Transformational leaders are likely to affect subordinates' perception of their work by making work appear more meaningful, thus increasing positive citizenship behaviors including peacemaking, conscientiousness, and meeting organizational objectives. Keller (2006) explains, "transformational leaders can create an impression that he or she has a high competence and a vision to achieve success. Subordinates respond with enthusiasm and commitment to the teams objectives" (p. 202). This concept is critical to success in an organization, as transformational leadership is known to produce more engaged, more devoted, and less self-centered employees who perform beyond the levels of set expectations (Bono & Judge, 2003).

Leadership in Action

Winston Churchill
Former Prime Minister of the UK

Winston Churchill is widely renowned as one of the most effective leaders in the history of the British government. Churchill found success as a leader because of not just what he did, but also who he was. His leadership style attempted to build morale in order to motivate his followers to achieve a common purpose. In short, he worked to inspire people. Churchill was known for visiting towns adversely affected by bombings during WWII. He utilized his "bigger than life" personality to convince people to remain optimistic about their potential to win the war. His optimism helped rally the public. In addition, his optimism allowed him to help initiate the "Big Three" Alliance between the UK, Russia and the U.S. Consequently, he helped lead to the "Big Three's" winning WWII. But nowhere was Churchill's inspirational nature more apparent than through his words, both written and spoken. Churchill was famous for creating inspiring calls to action during his speeches. In his two most famous speeches, "We Shall Fight on the Beaches" and "Finest Hour," Churchill projected an unbridled optimism in the face of remarkable obstacles. He delivered "We Shall Storm the Beaches" after the Allied Forces had just achieved the "Miracle of Dunkirk." However, the Allied command knew their position was precarious and that France could be the next country to fall. Churchill proceeded to offer a passionate rallying cry declaring to the Allied Forces (particularly American forces) that they would fight no matter where the battle took them and they would never surrender. Churchill continued to inject hope into the British people. In "Finest Hour," Churchill rallied both the British Parliament and the British people, painting a vivid picture of Britain as the last line of defense between Hitler and control of the European continent. Churchill reminded them that "the battle of Britain has just begun" and this would be Britain's finest hour. Churchill's optimism was the primary means by which he was able to motivate and inspire those around him to work towards common organizational goals.

8.8.2 Effective leaders focus on strengths

Effective leaders recognize that the most effective organizations understand and utilize their own strengths and the strengths of others. This thinking mirrors the work of Martin Seligman, which highlighted the thinking that organizational focus should shift from "what is wrong with people" (and, by proxy, what is wrong with the organization) to "what is right with people" (and the organization). In practice, this idea means that truly effective leaders are able to put their followers in positions to succeed by recognizing their strengths and then leveraging those strengths on their areas of expertise. This concept doesn't mean, however, that effective leaders don't challenge their followers to move outside of their comfort zones; rather, it means that effective leaders help their followers focus their efforts on areas that match their strengths—and offer them scaffolding to succeed if they are asked to operate outside their areas of strength. Indeed, the most effective leaders nurture their followers in ways that allow them to be the best versions of themselves.

Leadership in Action

Henry Ford
Founder, Ford Motor Company

Henry Ford was an extraordinary leader. Although Henry Ford is often credited with revolutionizing the auto industry, remarkably, he wasn't actually first to market. Other car companies actually beat Henry Ford to the punch, so to speak; however, Ford was extremely innovative, and he knew how to leverage the strengths of people within his organization to achieve maximum success. One of the most remarkable ways that Henry Ford was able to leverage his strengths—and the strengths of those who worked for him—is that he had an innate understanding of how best to motivate people to performing at their highest levels. Ford was revolutionary in that he paid his workers higher wages than average and took steps to reduce the hours they were required to work. This idea became a wildly effective strategy because it engendered a deep sense of loyalty in his employees. In addition, Ford was innovative in his willingness to hire women and minorities, offer health benefits, and champion LGBT rights. Ford famously said, "if there is any one secret of success, it lies in the ability to get the other person's point of view and see things from that person's angle, as well as your own." He recognized that the key to a successful organization was ensuring that employees recognize their own worth and their own strengths so they can reach achievement at the most optimal levels. Ford had a remarkable ability to not only identify his own strengths but also help his employees recognize their own strengths. This commitment to the betterment of his employees also caused them to be extremely loyal to Ford and the company.

8.8.3 Effective leaders articulate a clear vision

Vision is the compass that helps clearly delineate the organization's direction. Consequently, an effective leader must have a clear understanding of, and ability to articulate, their vision of the organization. As we discussed in earlier chapters, employees generally desire structure and tend to be goal, or mission, focused. A clear vision provides both organizational and individual focus. However, simply having a vision is not enough. Effective leaders constantly assess their organizational vision to ensure their organizations are operating, with intention, towards a common goal. This intentionality is important. Intentionality allows leaders to replicate success when it comes. If you know what you did to get there, your organization can keep moving in that direction to optimize success.

Leadership in Action

Walt Disney
Founder, Disney Company

Walt Disney is the founder of the world's most profitable and recognizable media company. Though the Disney corporation has now branched into a multitude of franchises and entertainment arenas, Walt Disney always approached the entertainment business with a singular focus. Walt Disney had a vision of what he wanted to create. When he bought swampland in Florida, people told him he was crazy. But he held firm to his vision. Walt Disney is also known for his collaborative style. Hundreds of images of Walt Disney show him huddled around a story board with other members of his team, offering input and advice to his artists and writers. Disney was uncompromising in his vision; whether it was a story, a movie or the experience that he wanted people to have at his theme parks, he refused to compromise. Nothing was impossible; they just hadn't figured out how to do it yet. In the throes of the Great Depression, Disney borrowed $1.5 million dollars to film the first full-length animated film, *Snow White and the Seven Dwarves*. People told him that adults would never sit through an animated feature film, but his commitment never wavered, and the film succeeded beyond expectations. Disney's commitment to the singular vision of making the impossible possible has inspired some of the greatest innovations in film and animation. Over three-fourths of Walt Disney Company employees cite that they are proud to be part of the company, and 67% are motivated by the company's mission, vision, and values—which is remarkable for a company in which almost 40% of the workforce are part time workers. As Walt Disney himself once said, "When you believe in a thing, believe in it all the way, implicitly and unquestionable."

8.8.4 Effective Leaders Create a Positive Culture

Organizational culture is extremely important to building consensus, and an effective leader will be aware of how individual motivations will affect the organization's culture. Organizational culture is unique because it often has to be created "at the top" but implemented among the "rank and file" members of the organization. Effective leaders understand the individuals within their organization so are mindful of how those individuals fit into the organization's broader tapestry. Effective leaders recognize how an individual's overall wellbeing can contribute to the effectiveness of the organization's culture. In "Leading from Within: The Effects of Emotion Recognition and Personality on Transformational Leadership Behavior", Bommer, et. al discuss the influence of a leaders' ability to understand and recognize employees' emotions. According to the authors, "a leader's ability to accurately recognize emotions in followers opens a window to followers authentic feelings. Emotion recognition involves the ability to accurately decode others expressions of emotions communicated through nonverbal channels" (Bommer, et. al, 2005, p. 847). A leaders' ability to accurately recognize emotion is critical if they hope to inspire followers and build relationships, particularly in a multigenerational workplace.

Leadership in Action

Dolly Parton
Singer, Songwriter, Actress, Founder, The Dollywood Company

Dolly Parton is a self-made success story and has built a multi-million-dollar entertainment empire through her hard work and determination. She has always connected with people, and her leadership style is noted for being rooted in her desire to make every person with whom she works feel like they are part of her family. Parton famously said, "find out who you are and do it on purpose." She has personified that mantra by establishing a set of values and then living out those values on a daily basis. She constantly seeks feedback about how and where the organization is headed. She has created an environment where her employees feel they can communicate honestly and their feedback will be valued and utilized to make the organization better. She has created a culture of honesty, and everyone in the organization is expected to act with honesty and integrity. Dolly Parton also believes in giving back. She regularly gives to charitable causes because she believes that if you are in a position of power then you should give back whatever you can. She has donated one million dollars to the Vanderbilt Children's Hospital and one million to help fund coronavirus research. Also, she created the Imagination Library which provides children with one free book per month from the time they are born until the time that they go to school. In 2018, her foundation had donated over 100,000,000 books! In addition, Parton has spoken publicly about the need to allow people in your organization to make mistakes. She has noted that leaders should not hold grudges because those grudges tend to make other people negative and ultimately impacts the team. If there is a culture where failure is embraced and built upon, then mistakes are not the end of the process but the beginning of learning. Finally, Parton has predicated all of her companies on loving the people around her. She emulates joy when around members of her team and recognizes how contagious positivity and love can be within an organization. She has spoken out on a number of social causes, from education disparities to the Black Lives Matter movement. She lives her commitment to love those around her. The positive attitude with which she operates her career and companies has made Dolly Parton one of the most influential and impactful people in the entertainment industry.

8.8.5 Effective leaders create inclusive workspaces

Effective leaders constantly work to evolve their organizations into places where individuals are free to be themselves and where their diversity and differences are not just accepted but celebrated. Truly inclusive workspaces are led by individuals who are not threatened when their point of view is challenged; rather, they embrace such disagreement as an opportunity for the organization to grow. Effective leaders recognize that differing perspectives are an avenue by which to develop strength rather than an indication of weakness. The ability to feel engaged, respected, and influential causes people to experience a sense of authenticity in their workplace. These feelings of authenticity allow people to find more satisfaction in their work, which, in turn, makes them more likely to feel connected to the organization—and thus increases their productivity.

Leadership in Action

Geraldine Huse
CEO & President of Proctor & Gamble, Canada

Geraldine Huse, and Proctor & Gamble as a company, has always been dedicated to the notion of diversity and inclusion. In order to accomplish her vision, Huse has been at the forefront of the company's push to encourage diversity of thought as one of their main principles. To achieve this goal, she encourages disagreements between members of the organization. She notes that "accessing diverse viewpoints is vital in creating optimum strategies and plans. An inclusive leader creates an environment where disagreement is viewed positively. I have learned from experience that the more diverse the team, the more debate and disagreement we have and the better the outcome." Huse intentionally searches out people who disagree with the direction and scope of the company's work. She believes that discoursing with those you disagree with enables closing some of the gaps in your organization. Nurturing disagreement allows people to move beyond the status quo and find solutions they may not have considered if only dealing with those who think the same way. While Huse has been a champion of the idea that diversity is much more than just the way a team looks, she also realizes that representation matters. She has consistently worked to ensure that women play prominent roles in her organization. She has created diversity training programs and made gender diversity one of the hallmarks of her career. However, she recognizes that it isn't just the existence of diversity that will improve an organization. She has noted that "diversity is a measure. Inclusion is a skill." The goal is to create a workplace where people are able to be their authentic selves and their contributions are valued and appreciated. She believes that concept means that the people in charge have to live that inclusivity both inside and outside of work. It has to extend to the way that their team members think. Huse has worked tirelessly to create a team with people who solve problems in different ways, think about the world from a myriad of different perspectives, and champion varying approaches to challenges, and this has led to her being one of the most successful CEOs in the Proctor & Gamble company's history.

8.8.6 Effective leaders operate in an ethical manner

Effective leaders lead with integrity. Ethical leaders are conscientious, inclusive, accountable, considerate, and consistent. Ethical leaders who encourage loyalty and reduce conflict are more likely to win over a multigenerational workforce. They tend to operate from a place of honesty. They are up front with their key stakeholders, and their word tends to operate as their bond. However, ethical leadership is not only about the behavior of those who are in charge. Ethical leadership allows for a culture of trust within the workplace where people feel free to complete tasks without the threat of micromanagement (which fosters a pervasive culture where there is a lack of trust within the workplace). Ethical leadership requires open communication and a willingness of those in charge to listen to those with whom they work. The most effective ethical leaders have mastered these techniques to increase overall productivity within their organizations.

Leadership in Action

Ed Stack
Chairman & CEO, Dick's Sporting Goods

Many people say that tragedy defines a person. In this instance, tragedy (or a series of tragedies) caused Dick's Sporting Goods to reevaluate their policies. CEO Ed Stack began to notice that there were increasing gun related tragedies happening in schools across America. And in 2012, after the Sandy Hook Elementary school shooting, Stack knew he needed to do what he considered to be the right thing. He decided that the sporting goods chain needed to reevaluate the way they sold guns. He contacted stores personally, explaining that there was going to be a shift in policy, and he was honest and up front about the reasons why. He mandated that all AR-15 semiautomatic rifles be removed from all stores across the country. This change came without any major announcement, and the company faced significant backlash from the broader community. Stack stood firm in the face of criticism and was willing to answer questions from the media and his critics. When faced with an N.R.A. backed boycott, Stack committed to destroying all of the company's assault style rifles (approximately five million dollars' worth of products). After the 2018 shooting at Marjory Stoneman Douglass High School in Parkland, Florida, Stack instituted even more stringent policies, announcing that Dick's Sporting Goods would no longer sell firearms to anyone under the age of 21. This decision was not an easy one, and Stack estimates it cost the company close to $250,000,000 in annual sales. However, he is convinced that he did the right thing. Stack noted, "so many people say to me, you know, 'if we do what you want to do, it's not going to stop these mass shootings' and my response is you're probably right, it won't. But if we do these things and it saves one life, don't you think it's worth it?" He believed he had an obligation, as a leader with influence, to step up and take the lead. He notes that he never set out to be an activist; he simply wanted to do what's right. Stack has operated with integrity and convinced the members of his leadership team that doing what's right is, at times, more important than the bottom line.

8.9 SUMMARY

All of the profiles explored in this chapter illustrate leaders who were able to find great success despite their varied approaches to effective leadership. That is because leadership is not a one size fits all enterprise; rather, it is developed over time and is most effective when tailored to the particular individual who is being asked to lead. Think of effective leadership as a roadmap. A map shows various paths to any single destination. It isn't that one route is necessarily better than the others; instead, each route presents its own challenges and opportunities. Effective leaders figure out the best route for their organization and empower those who are following them to achieve both their personal, and the organization's overall, goals.

8.10 DISCUSSION QUESTIONS

1. What are some ways that organizations can work to improve employee engagement? What do you believe is the most effective method and why?

2. Find a leader not mentioned in this book who fits the profiles below. Explain why this particular style helped them to be an effective leader.

   a. Creating Inclusive Workspaces

   b. Ethical Leadership

   c. Creating a Positive Culture

   d. Developing People's Strengths

3. Research has showed that effective leadership is linked to mental and physical wellbeing. Which of these is more important? Describe the impact that a lack of resources could have on an organization.

4. Choose a leader whom you believe is effective. What makes them so effective? What leadership style best describes how they operate? How could you adapt some of those characteristics in creating your own leadership style?

8.11 REFERENCES

Bolman, L.G. and Deal, T.E. (2017). *Reframing Organizations: Artistry, Choice, and Leadership.* John Wiley and Sons, Inc.

Bono, Joyce E., and Timothy A. Judge. 2003. "Self-Concordance at Work: Toward Understanding the Motivational Effects of Transformational Leaders." Academy of Management Journal 46 (5): 554–71. doi:10.5465/30040649.

Cropanzano, Russell,Rupp, Deborah E.,Byrne, Zinta S. Journal of Applied Psychology, Vol 88(1), Feb 2003, 160-169.

Fisher, Jim. 2016. The Thoughtful Leader : A Model of Integrative Leadership. Toronto: Rotman-UTP Publishing. http://search.ebscohost.com/login.aspx?direct=true&AuthType=ip,shib&db=nlebk&AN=1287413&site=eds-live&scope=site.

Gilbreath B, and Benson PG. 2004. "The Contribution of Supervisor Behaviour to Employee Psychological Well-Being." Work & Stress 18 (3): 255–66.

https://www.mayoclinic.org/healthy-lifestyle/adult-health/in-depth/burnout/art-20046642

https://www.workplacestrategiesformentalhealth.com/psychological-health-and-safety/relevant-statistics#

https://www.workplacestrategiesformentalhealth.com/psychological-health-and-safety/relevant-statistics#

https://www.who.int/mental_health/in_the_workplace/en/

https://blog.smarp.com/employee-engagement-8-statistics-you-need-to-know

https://www.zenefits.com/workest/employee-turnover-infographic/

https://www.conference-board.org/topics/dna-of-engagement

http://news.gallup.com/businessjournal/163130/employee-engagement-drives-growth.aspx

https://www.octanner.com/insights/articles/2019/11/13/what_kind_of_company.html

https://www.resourcefulmanager.com/guides/successful-leaders/

https://www.michaelleestallard.com/leading-with-character-integrity http://search.ebscohost.com/login.aspx?direct=true&AuthType=ip,shib&db=edsjsr&AN=edsjsr.4093953&site=eds-live&scope=site.

http://search.ebscohost.com/login.aspx?direct=true&AuthType=ip,shib&db=edsovi&AN=edsovi.00004565.200601000.00018&site=eds-live&scope=site.

http://search.ebscohost.com/login.aspx?direct=true&AuthType=ip,shib&db=nlebk&AN=1287413&site=eds-live&scope=site.

http://search.ebscohost.com/login.aspx?direct=true&AuthType=ip,shib&db=ccm&AN=106623773&site=eds-live&scope=site.

http://search.ebscohost.com/login.aspx?direct=true&AuthType=ip,shib&db=nlebk&AN=944497&site=eds-live&scope=site.

https://www.smithsonianmag.com/history/winston-churchills-historic-fight-them-beaches-speech-wasnt-heard-public-until-after-wwii-180967278/.

http://search.ebscohost.com/login.aspx?direct=true&AuthType=ip,shib&db=nlebk&AN=148477&site=eds-live&scope=site.

Neuschel, Robert P., and Kellogg School of Management. 2005. The Servant Leader: Unleashing the Power of Your People. Evanston, Ill: Kogan Page.

PICCOLO, RONALD F., and JASON A. COLQUITT. 2006. "Transformational Leadership and Job Behaviors: The Mediating Role of Core Job Characteristics." Academy of Management Journal 49 (2): 327–40. doi:10.5465/AMJ.2006.20786079.

Robert T., Keller. 2006. "Transformational Leadership, Initiating Structure, and Substitutes for Leadership: A Longitudinal Study of Research and Development Project Team Performance." Journal of Applied Psychology, no. 1: 202.

Schroth, H. (2019). Are You Ready for Gen Z in the Workplace? California Management Review, 61(3), 5–18. https://doi.org/10.1177/0008125619841006.

Sy, Thomas, Stéphane Côté, and Richard Saavedra. 2005. "The Contagious Leader: Impact of the Leader's Mood on the Mood of Group Members, Group Affective Tone, and Group Processes." Journal of Applied Psychology 90 (2): 295–305. doi:10.1037/0021-9010.90.2.295.

Tepper, Bennett J., Michelle K. Duffy, Christine A. Henle, and Lisa Schurer Lambert. 2006. "Procedural Injustice, Victim Precipitation, and Abusive Supervision." Personnel Psychology 59 (1): 101–23. doi:10.1111/j.1744-6570.2006.00725.x.

van Dierendonck, Dirk, Clare Haynes, Carol Borrill, and Chris Stride. 2004. "Leadership Behavior and Subordinate Well-Being." Journal of Occupational Health Psychology 9 (2): 165–75. doi:10.1037/1076-8998.9.2.165.

William H. Bommer, Gregory A. Rich, and Robert S. Rubin. 2005. "Changing Attitudes about Change: Longitudinal Effects of Transformational Leader Behavior on Employee Cynicism about Organizational Change." Journal of Organizational Behavior 26 (7): 733. http://search.ebscohost.com/login.aspx?direct=true&AuthType=ip,shib&db=edsjsr&AN=edsjsr.4093953&site=eds-live&scope=site.

www.ingramcontent.com/pod-product-compliance
Lightning Source LLC
Chambersburg PA
CBHW050749100426
42744CB00012BA/1944